$42.40

GO!

with Microsoft®

Office 365

Getting Started

Shelley Gaskin and Robert L. Ferrett

PEARSON

Boston   Columbus   Indianapolis   New York   San Francisco   Upper Saddle River
Amsterdam   Cape Town   Dubai   London   Madrid   Milan   Munich   Paris   Montreal   Toronto
Delhi   Mexico City   São Paulo   Sydney   Hong Kong   Seoul   Singapore   Taipei   Tokyo

Editor in Chief: Michael Payne
Executive Editor: Jenifer Niles
Product Development Manager: Laura Burgess
Senior Editorial Project Manager: Meghan Bisi
Editorial Assistant: Carly Prakapas
VP/Director of Business & Technology Marketing: Patrice Lumumba Jones
Marketing Coordinator: Susan Osterlitz
Marketing Assistant: Darshika Vyas
Associate Managing Editor: Camille Trentacoste
Senior Production Project Manager: Rhonda Aversa
Operations Specialist: Maura Zaldivar-Garcia

Senior Operation Manager/Site Lead: Nick Sklitsis
Senior Art Director: Jonathan Boylan
Cover Photo: © Ben Durrant
Associate Director of Design: Blair Brown
Director of Media Development: Cathi Profitko
Senior Media Project Manager, Editorial: Alana Coles
Media Project Manager, Production: John Cassar
Full-Service Project Management: PreMediaGlobal
Composition: PreMediaGlobal
Printer/Binder: Courier Kendallville
Cover Printer: Lehigh-Phoenix Color/Hagerstown
Text Font: Minion Pro

Credits and acknowledgments borrowed from other sources and reproduced, with permission, in this textbook appear on the appropriate page within text.

Microsoft and/or its respective suppliers make no representations about the suitability of the information contained in the documents and related graphics published as part of the services for any purpose. All such documents and related graphics are provided "as is" without warranty of any kind. Microsoft and/or its respective suppliers hereby disclaim all warranties and conditions with regard to this information, including all warranties and conditions of merchantability, whether express, implied or statutory, fitness for a particular purpose, title and non-infringement. In no event shall microsoft and/or its respective suppliers be liable for any special, indirect or consequential damages or any damages whatsoever resulting from loss of use, data or profits, whether in an action of contract, negligence or other tortious action, arising out of or in connection with the use or performance of information available from the services.

The documents and related graphics contained herein could include technical inaccuracies or typographical errors. Changes are periodically added to the information herein. Microsoft and/or its respective suppliers may make improvements and/or changes in the product(s) and/or the program(s) described herein at any time.

Microsoft® and Windows® are registered trademarks of the Microsoft Corporation in the U.S.A. and other countries. This book is not sponsored or endorsed by or affiliated with the Microsoft Corporation.

Many of the designations by manufacturers and sellers to distinguish their products are claimed as trademarks. Where those designations appear in this book, and the publisher was aware of a trademark claim, the designations have been printed in initial caps or all caps.

Library of Congress Cataloging-in-Publication Data

Gaskin, Shelley.
  GO! with Microsoft Office 365 : getting started / Shelley Gaskin and Robert L. Ferrett Pearson.
    p. cm.
  Includes index.
  ISBN 978-0-13-295574-4 (alk. paper) — ISBN 978-0-13-295576-8 (coursesmart)
  1. Microsoft Office. 2. Business—Computer programs. I. Ferrett, Robert. II. Title.
  HF5548.4.M525G3667 2013
  005.5—dc23

                                        2012006461

10 9 8 7 6 5 4 3 2 1

ISBN-10: 0-13-295574-1
ISBN-13: 978-0-13-295574-4

Contents

About the Authors

Shelley Gaskin, Series Editor, is a professor in the Business and Computer Technology Division at Pasadena City College in Pasadena, California. She holds a bachelor's degree in Business Administration from Robert Morris College (Pennsylvania), a master's degree in Business from Northern Illinois University, and a doctorate in Adult and Community Education from Ball State University. Before joining Pasadena City College, she spent 12 years in the computer industry where she was a systems analyst, sales representative, and Director of Customer Education with Unisys Corporation. She also worked for Ernst & Young on the development of large systems applications for their clients. She has written and developed training materials for custom systems applications in both the public and private sector, and has written and edited numerous computer application textbooks.

This book is dedicated to my students, who inspire me every day.

Robert L. Ferrett recently retired as the Director of the Center for Instructional Computing at Eastern Michigan University, where he provided computer training and support to faculty. He has authored or co-authored more than 70 books on Access, PowerPoint, Excel, Publisher, WordPerfect, Windows, Word, OpenOffice, and Computer Fundamentals. He has been designing, developing, and delivering computer workshops for more than three decades. Before writing for the *GO! Series*, Bob was a series editor for the Learn Series. He has a bachelor's degree in Psychology, a master's degree in Geography, and a master's degree in Interdisciplinary Technology from Eastern Michigan University. His doctoral studies were in Instructional Technology at Wayne State University.

I'd like to dedicate this book to my wife Mary Jane,
whose constant support has been so important all these years.

Teach the Course You Want in Less Time

A Microsoft® Office textbook designed for student success!

- **Project-Based –** Students learn by creating projects that they will use in the real world.

- **Microsoft Procedural Syntax –** Steps are written to put students in the right place at the right time.

- **Teachable Moment –** Expository text is woven into the steps—at the moment students need to know it—not chunked together in a block of text that will go unread.

- **Sequential Pagination –** Students have actual page numbers instead of confusing letters and abbreviations.

Student Outcomes and Learning Objectives – Objectives are clustered around projects that result in student outcomes.

Project Activities – A project summary stated clearly and quickly.

Project Files – Clearly shows students which files are needed for the project and the names they will use to save their documents.

Scenario – Each chapter opens with a story that sets the stage for the projects the student will create.

Project Results – Shows students how their final outcome will appear.

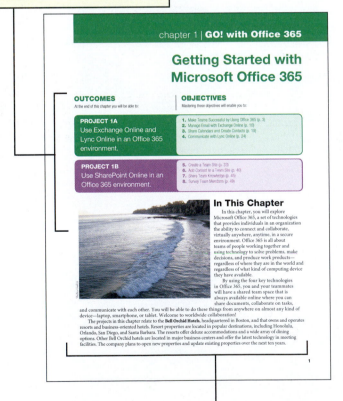

Color Coding – Color variations between the two projects in each chapter make it easy to identify which project students are working on.

Microsoft Procedural Syntax – Steps are written to put the student in the right place at the right time.

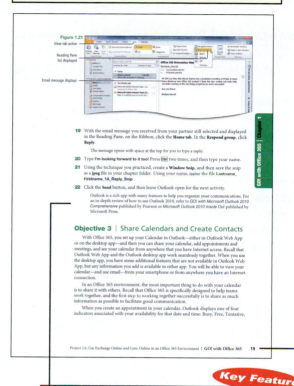

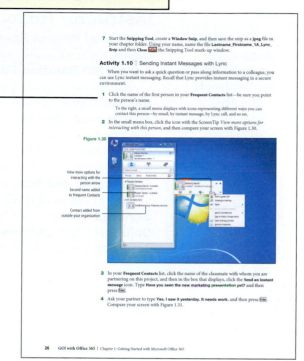

Teachable Moment – Expository text is woven into the steps—at the moment students need to know it—not chunked together in a block of text that will go unread.

Sequential Pagination – Students are given actual page numbers to navigate through the textbook instead of confusing letters and abbreviations.

End-of-Chapter

Content-Based Assessments – Assessments with defined solutions.

Student Resources

Companion Website – Student Data Files, the Online Study Guide (an interactive quiz), and a Glossary are at www.pearsonhighered.com/go.

Instructor Resources

Additional Project Exams (formerly Point-Counted Production Tests) – provided by chapter, application, and project with a scorecard for easy grading.

Annotated Solution Files – Coupled with the scorecards, these create a grading and scoring system that makes grading so much easier for you.

Answer Key – Answers to end-of-chapter questions.

Assignment Sheets – Lists all the assignments for the chapter. Just add in the course information, due dates, and points. Providing these to students ensures they will know what is due and when.

Image Library – A library of all the figures from the book.

PowerPoint Lectures – PowerPoint presentations for each chapter.

Scorecards and Scoring Rubrics – Can be used by either students to check their work or by instructors as a quick check-off for the items that need to be corrected.

Scripted Lectures – Classroom lectures prepared for you.

Solution Files and Solution PDFs – The student's completed file.

Test Bank – Includes a variety of test questions for each chapter.

All Instructor materials available on the IRC

Getting Started with Microsoft Office 365

OUTCOMES
At the end of this chapter you will be able to:

OBJECTIVES
Mastering these objectives will enable you to:

PROJECT 1A
Use Exchange Online and Lync Online in an Office 365 environment.

1. Make Teams Successful by Using Office 365 (p. 3)
2. Manage Email with Exchange Online (p. 10)
3. Share Calendars and Create Contacts (p. 19)
4. Communicate with Lync Online (p. 24)

PROJECT 1B
Use SharePoint Online in an Office 365 environment.

5. Create a Team Site (p. 33)
6. Add Content to a Team Site (p. 40)
7. Share Team Knowledge (p. 45)
8. Survey Team Members (p. 49)

Shelley Gaskin

In This Chapter

In this chapter, you will explore Microsoft Office 365, a set of technologies that provides individuals in an organization the ability to connect and collaborate, virtually anywhere, anytime, in a secure environment. Office 365 is all about teams of people working together and using technology to solve problems, make decisions, and produce work products—regardless of where they are in the world and regardless of what kind of computing device they have available.

By using the four key technologies in Office 365, you and your teammates will have a shared team space that is always available online where you can share documents, collaborate on tasks, and communicate with each other. You will be able to do these things from anywhere on almost any kind of device—laptop, smartphone, or tablet. Welcome to worldwide collaboration!

The projects in this chapter relate to the **Bell Orchid Hotels**, headquartered in Boston, and that owns and operates resorts and business-oriented hotels. Resort properties are located in popular destinations, including Honolulu, Orlando, San Diego, and Santa Barbara. The resorts offer deluxe accommodations and a wide array of dining options. Other Bell Orchid hotels are located in major business centers and offer the latest technology in meeting facilities. The company plans to open new properties and update existing properties over the next ten years.

Project 1A Use Exchange Online and Lync Online in an Office 365 Environment

Project Activities

In Activities 1.01 through 1.12, you will use Microsoft Outlook in an Exchange Online environment for email and contacts. By using Lync Online, you will communicate with instant messaging, conduct a video call, and take control of another teammate's computer screen. As you work, you will capture six screens that will look similar to Figure 1.1.

Project Files

For Project 1A, you will need the following file:

o01A_Marketing_Presentation

You will save your files as:

Lastname_Firstname_1A_Email_Snip
Lastname_Firstname_1A_Reply_Snip
Lastname_Firstname_1A_Calendar_Snip
Lastname_Firstname_1A_Contact_Snip
Lastname_Firstname_1A_Lync_Snip
Lastname_Firstname_1A_Video_Snip

Project Results

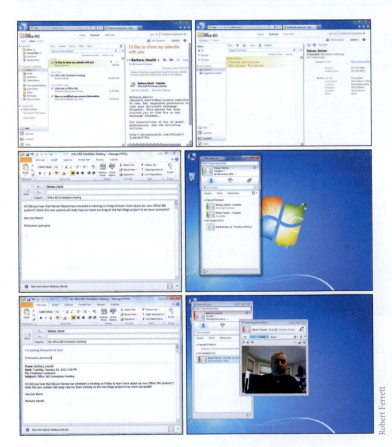

Robert Ferrett

Figure 1.1

Objective 1 | Make Teams Successful by Using Office 365

In every job, you must work and communicate with other people. A group of workers tasked with working together to solve a problem, make a decision, or create a work product is referred to as a *team*. For a team to succeed, the team members must be able to communicate with each other easily.

If all the team members work at the same location and work the same hours, communication is easy. You schedule face-to-face meetings and exchange documents and information among yourselves. But that is a rare arrangement in today's organizations. Rather, it is more likely that the members of your team work in different locations—even different countries—and work different hours or travel extensively away from the headquarters location. Also, for specific projects, teams are frequently organized across different departments of an organization or even across different organizations entirely. Then when the project is complete, the team disbands.

Collaboration is when you work together with others as a team in an intellectual endeavor to complete a shared task or achieve a shared goal; for example, when you and one or more of your classmates work together on a class project. Collaboration involves giving feedback to and receiving feedback from others on the team, and then revising the strategies to achieve the goal or to produce the work product based on the feedback.

Microsoft Office 365, the system you will learn about in this text, will help your team work together and collaborate in a manner that produces a work product that is better than any single individual on the team could produce by working alone.

> **Alert!** | To complete this chapter, beginning with Activity 1.06, you will need access to an Office 365 site.
>
> Activities 1.01 through 1.05 will help you understand the Office 365 environment by reading and answering questions about Office 365. The hands-on portion of the instruction begins with Activity 1.06, at which point, you must have, or your instructor must provide you, access to an Office 365 site and an appropriate User ID and password.

Activity 1.01 | Understanding Microsoft Office 365

Microsoft Office 365 is a set of secure online services that enables people in an organization to communicate and collaborate by using any Internet-connected device—a computer, a tablet, or a smartphone. Because Office 365 offers access from anywhere to email, Web conferencing, documents, and calendars, everyone on a team can work together easily. *Office 365 is intended for use by multiple users in an organization* and is offered on a monthly subscription basis to organizations starting as low as $6 per month per user.

Office 365 combines tools for collaboration and productivity and delivers them to multiple users in an organization by using *cloud computing*—the ability to access files and software applications online with multiple devices. For example, one cloud service with which you might be familiar is *Windows Live SkyDrive* as shown in Figure 1.2, a free Web-based application with which you can save, store, organize, and share files online.

Figure 1.2

Links to Office Web Apps
to create Word, Excel,
PowerPoint, or
OneNote files

Windows live SkyDrive
for an employee with
Bell Orchid Hotels

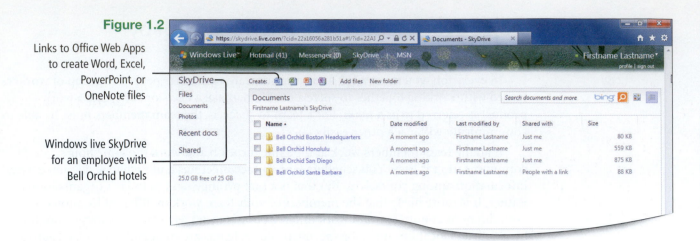

Another cloud service from Microsoft is *Office Web Apps*, one of which is shown in Figure 1.3. These applications are the online companions to the desktop versions of Microsoft Office Word, Excel, PowerPoint, and OneNote that enable you to create, access, share, and perform light editing on Microsoft Office documents from any device that connects to the Internet and uses a supported *Web browser*. A Web browser is software, such as Internet Explorer, Firefox, Safari, or Chrome, that displays Web pages.

Figure 1.3

A new document in
Word Web App

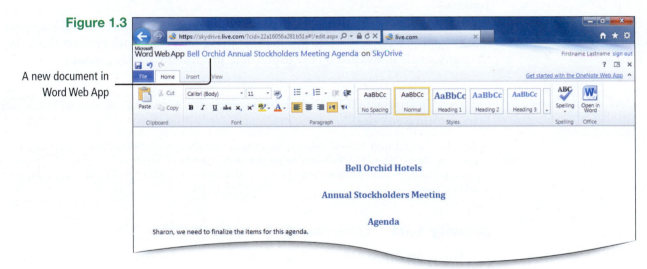

For an organization, cloud computing enables the addition of services without investing in additional hardware and software. For you as a team member, you can simply use your Web browser to access, edit, store, and share files.

To check how well you understand working with a team and what Office 365 is, take a moment to answer the following questions:

1 For a team to succeed, the team members must be able to _____ with each other easily.

2 Collaboration involves giving and receiving _____.

3 Collaboration typically produces a work product that is better than any single individual could produce by working _____.

4 Office 365 is intended for use by _____ users in an organization.

5 Office 365 is delivered by using _____ computing.

Activity 1.02 | Understanding Security in Office 365

Office 365 includes business-class security and is backed by Microsoft. For an organization, what does that mean?

When you and a few classmates work together on a class project, you are not concerned about the security of your data. You probably use free personal email services such as Hotmail, Gmail, or Yahoo! Mail to exchange documents, or perhaps you post your documents to free services such as Google Docs.

Organizations, on the other hand—even small ones with only two or three employees—must be concerned with the privacy and security of their data. Organizations cannot entrust their data and confidential communications to free services that may change frequently or that have no legal responsibility for the security of the data.

Organizations must provide each employee with a company email address rather than having each employee use his or her own personal free email address for business communications. Organizations must provide a central storage location for its data rather than having employees store data on flash drives or local hard drives with no control or oversight.

An organization must have a *secure environment*, which is a system that uses controlled *servers*—computers that provide services on a network such as an email server or a file server—to ensure the security and privacy of email, to control the storage and use of information, and to protect against the loss of confidential data.

Most small organizations cannot afford to hire the people with the skills necessary to install and maintain servers. So to establish and maintain a secure environment, many small organizations contract with and rely on small IT—the acronym for *Information Technology*—hosting companies to host their email communications and to provide secure storage. For a fee, the IT hosting company *hosts*—provides, runs, and maintains any necessary servers—an organization's data to maintain a secure environment for the organization's networked computers. These contracts can be costly, and verifying the reputation of hosting companies can be time-consuming.

When you use Office 365, your email and storage servers are hosted by Microsoft. Your organization gets business-class security from Microsoft—a large, well-established company. Sophisticated security and data management features are built into Office 365 so that you can control *permissions*—access rights that define the ability of an individual or group to view or make changes to documents—and provide secure email and communications.

To check how well you understand security in Office 365, take a moment to answer the following questions:

1 Even small organizations must be concerned about the _____ and _____ of their data.

2 Free services probably have no _____ responsibility for the security of data.

3 Organizations must provide each employee with a company _____ address.

4 Most small organizations cannot afford to hire people with the skills necessary to install and maintain _____.

5 IT is an acronym for _____ _____.

Activity 1.03 | Communicating and Sharing with Office 365

To support the way individuals work together toward a common goal, Office 365 includes four key technologies for communication and productivity:

Microsoft Exchange Online provides email, contacts, calendars, and task scheduling to an organization's employees. There is no need to purchase, install, and maintain a mail server—Microsoft does that for you as part of Office 365. Microsoft maintains your mail server on a computer in one of its data centers. Before Office 365, it was expensive for small organizations to buy and maintain the Microsoft Exchange Server hardware and software necessary to provide business-class email and calendar sharing for employees.

Microsoft Lync Online is the instant messaging, audio/video calling, and online meeting tool in Office 365. Lync Online provides instant messaging—known as *IM*—and online meetings in a secure environment. There are free IM programs available, but because free programs are not based in a secure environment, they are not suitable for instant messaging among the employees of an organization who may be discussing confidential information about products or customers. Before Office 365, organizations could buy and install Lync server hardware and software, but doing so was expensive and time consuming for small organizations that could not afford full-time IT support.

Microsoft SharePoint Online provides document sharing and *team sites*, which are internal Web sites to share documents with others in an organization, manage documents, and publish reports for others to see. The advantage to using team sites is that you need only an Internet connection and a Web browser to view, interact with, and build content on a team site. Before Office 365, organizations could purchase and install SharePoint server hardware and software, but doing so was expensive and required an IT person to support the installation.

Office Web Apps provide the online companions to the desktop versions of Microsoft Office Word, Excel, PowerPoint, and OneNote that enable you to create, access, share, and perform light editing on Microsoft Office documents from any device that connects to the Internet and uses a supported Web browser. Office Web Apps are included as part of Office 365; however, you can also use your own installation of Microsoft Office.

Working with a team will probably be an important part of your future work life. As you progress in your career, you might be part of a team for a specific project or as part of a department or a special program. To succeed, you will need a team space to enable remote team members to access files, to provide a way to assign and share tasks and appointments and notes, to have an online meeting space for groups to call in to, or to meet as a group. And, you will need to be able to access and use this team space from multiple devices such as a smartphones, tablets, or laptop computers.

To check how well you understand sharing and communicating in Office 365, take a moment to answer the following questions:

1 _____ key technologies comprise Office 365.

2 Before Office 365, to have Microsoft business-class email, an organization would have to purchase and install hardware and software known as _____ _____ _____.

3 IM is the acronym for _____ _____.

4 Free IM programs are not suitable for an organization because they are not based in a _____ _____.

5 The advantage to using team sites is that you need only an _____ _____ and a _____ _____ to view, interact with, and build content on the site.

Activity 1.04 | Installing and Configuring Office 365

The advantage of using Office 365 is that your organization does not have to purchase and install server hardware and software for sophisticated business applications and does not need a full-time IT person or staff just to manage the technology your teams need.

By using Office 365, you are able to have business-class services for your employees without investing in expensive hardware, software, and personnel. However, at least one person in an organization must be designated as the *Office 365 Administrator*—the person who creates and manages the account, adds new users, sets up the services your organization wants to use, sets permission levels, and manages the SharePoint team sites. You can have more than one Administrator if you want to share these tasks with others.

Microsoft provides easy-to-use instructions and videos to get you started, and you might also have contact with a Microsoft representative. You will probably find, however, that subscribing to and setting up the account, adding users, and activating services is a straightforward process that requires little or no assistance.

After purchasing the required number of licenses, you will add each team member as a user that includes his or her email address. The first time you sign in as the Administrator, your screen will resemble Figure 1.4.

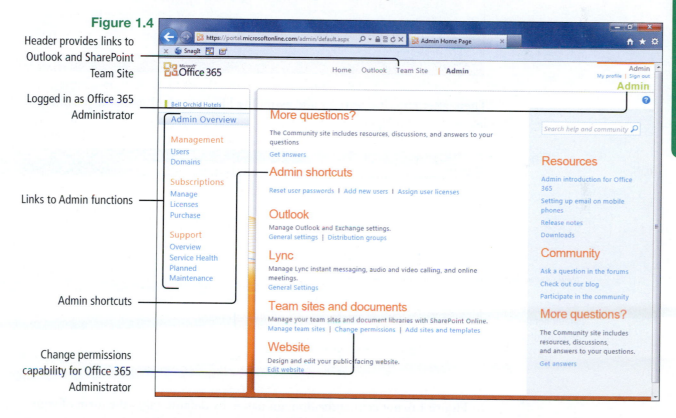

Figure 1.4

Header provides links to Outlook and SharePoint Team Site

Logged in as Office 365 Administrator

Links to Admin functions

Admin shortcuts

Change permissions capability for Office 365 Administrator

To add a new user, the system will walk you through five steps. First, you enter the Details for the new user, as shown in Figure 1.5.

GO! with Office 365 | Chapter 1

Figure 1.5

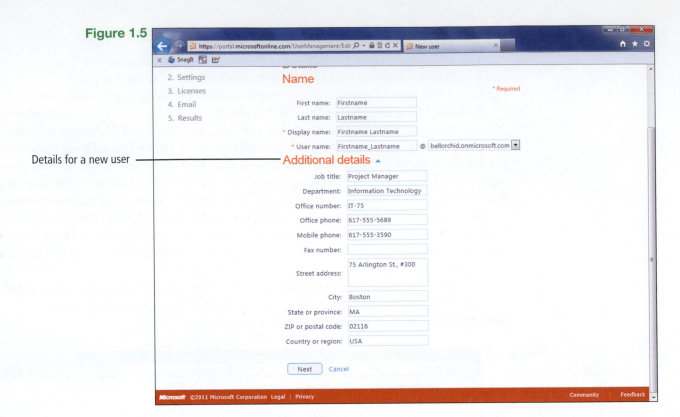

Details for a new user

Figure 1.6

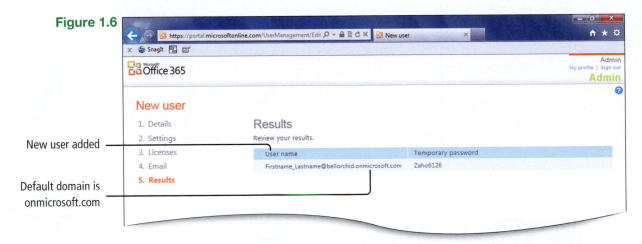

New user added

Default domain is onmicrosoft.com

Then, after entering Settings and assigning Licenses and Email, the Results will display as shown in Figure 1.6.

In Figure 1.6, notice that the domain name, by default, takes the form of your company name followed by *onmicrosoft.com*. For example, here the domain name is *bellorchid.onmicrosoft.com*. However, if your company has a registered domain name, you can easily add it by using the Add A Domain feature.

As the Administrator, you can view a list of all the Office 365 users you have added, as shown in Figure 1.7. Notice that the panel on the left assists you with things you might want to do as the Administrator.

Figure 1.7

Signed in as Admin

List of Admin functions

List of licensed users in the Admin view

As a new Office 365 user, your Administrator will inform you about your User ID and password, and the first time you sign in, your screen will resemble Figure 1.8.

Figure 1.8

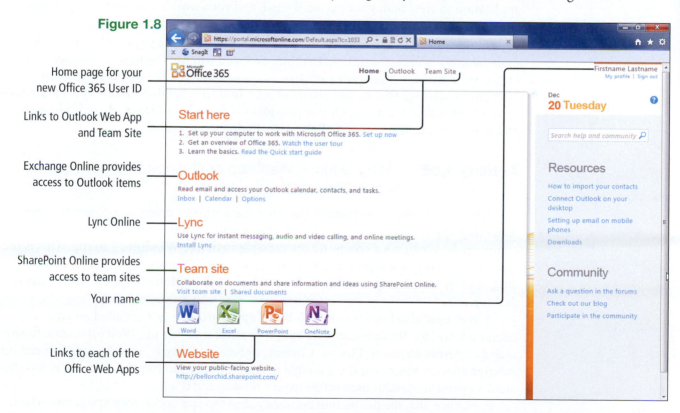

Home page for your new Office 365 User ID

Links to Outlook Web App and Team Site

Exchange Online provides access to Outlook items

Lync Online

SharePoint Online provides access to team sites

Your name

Links to each of the Office Web Apps

To check how well you understand installing and configuring Office 365, take a moment to answer the following questions:

1 The advantage of using Office 365 is that your organization does not have to purchase and install _____ hardware and software for sophisticated business applications.

2 The Office 365 Administrator is the person who creates and manages the _____.

3 After purchasing the required number of licenses, each member of an organization is added as a user that includes an _____ address.

4 By default, Office 365 creates a domain name consisting of your organization name followed by the text _____.

5 If your company has a _____ domain name, you can easily add it by using the Add A Domain feature.

Objective 2 | Manage Email with Exchange Online

You will use Microsoft Outlook to manage your email in an Office 365 environment. For your personal email on your own computer, you can use Outlook as a standalone email application. For example, if you have Microsoft Office installed on your computer, it includes Outlook, and you can use Outlook to view and organize your email from free Web-based email services such as Hotmail, Windows Live Mail, Gmail, or other free email services that are *POP3* or *IMAP* accounts. POP3 is a common protocol used to retrieve email messages from an Internet email server. IMAP is a protocol that creates folders on a server to store and organize messages for retrieval by other computers.

Many individuals use Outlook as a standalone application in this manner, and it is especially useful, because you can have multiple email accounts feed into your Outlook program. For example, on your own computer, you can use Outlook as a standalone application to view both your personal email and your work email—or your personal email from a Hotmail account and from a Gmail account.

On the other hand, recall that the purpose of Office 365 is to provide services for *multiple users in an organization*. In Office 365, you will use Outlook to manage your Office 365 email as a Microsoft Exchange account—not a POP3 or IMAP account. Microsoft Exchange Online and SharePoint Online are intended for use by *multiple users in an organization*. Exchange Online provides for shared mailboxes, shared calendars, and setting up meetings among all the users in the organization.

Activity 1.05 | Using Outlook Web App or Outlook Desktop App for Office 365 Email

App—the shortened version of the word *application*—refers to a computer program. A *desktop app* is a computer program that is installed on the hard drive of your computer and requires a computer operating system like Windows 7 to run. This is the type of app that you are probably most familiar with. The programs in Microsoft Office 2010 such as Word and Excel are desktop apps. Adobe's Photoshop is another common desktop app.

A *Web app*, also known as a *Web-based application*, is not installed on your computer, and for the application to run, it requires that you use Web browser software such as Internet Explorer, Firefox, Chrome, or Safari. Similarly, *mobile apps* that run on smartphones or tablets require a mobile operating system to run; for example iOS is the mobile operating system used on the Apple iPhone and iPad.

For Office 365, the distinction between a desktop app and a Web app is important, because you can use both Microsoft Office desktop apps with Office 365 and Microsoft's Office Web Apps with Office 365. Which one you use depends primarily on what you have available to you at the time you want to use the app.

For example, if you are an accountant for an organization like Bell Orchid Hotels, you probably spend most of your time at your office computer, and that computer likely has the full desktop version of Microsoft Office installed. When you are working at that computer, you can use the more powerful desktop versions of Microsoft Office—including Outlook. But when you travel on business, for example to visit one of the hotel properties in another city, you might take a laptop computer with you, and it may not have Microsoft Office 2010 installed.

If you are using a computer that does not have Microsoft Office 2010 installed, you can use your Web browser to view and edit Excel worksheets by using Excel Web App—the online companion to the desktop version of Microsoft Excel. Likewise, you can use Outlook Web App—the online companion to the desktop version of Microsoft Outlook—to view and respond to email if you are using a computer that does not have Microsoft Office 2010 installed.

By default, Office 365 uses the Outlook Web App. However, if the computer you are using has Office 2010 installed, you will probably want to set up your system to use the desktop app, which has more features. Likewise, you will probably want to use the other Microsoft Office 2010 desktop apps if they are installed on your computer.

People use email at work every day—it is the most common form of communication in the workplace. With Office 365, you can use Outlook Web App, or Outlook on the desktop, or both. Outlook Web App is streamlined and focused on the most common Outlook features. It also enables you to view your email on a mobile device.

Outlook 2010 on the desktop has additional features that are not available in Outlook Web App. For example, in the desktop app, you can use *Conversation View* to see email threads in a condensed format. When Conversations is turned on, messages that share the same Subject appear in a group. You also get Mail Tips to help you avoid mistakes such as clicking Reply All to a long list of people.

You can switch seamlessly between Outlook Web App and the Outlook desktop app. The one you use will depend on where you are and what device you have in your hand.

Figure 1.9 displays how your screen will look when you click Outlook immediately after your Office 365 User ID is set up. This is Outlook Web App.

Figure 1.9

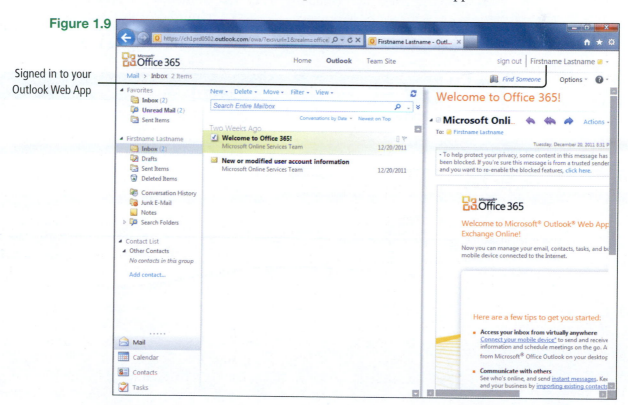

Signed in to your Outlook Web App

To finish setting up your computer for Office 365, you will want to follow the steps to install Lync and to set up and configure your Office desktop apps, as shown in Figure 1.10. Note that to accomplish these tasks, you must be signed on to your Windows account as an Administrator.

Figure 1.10

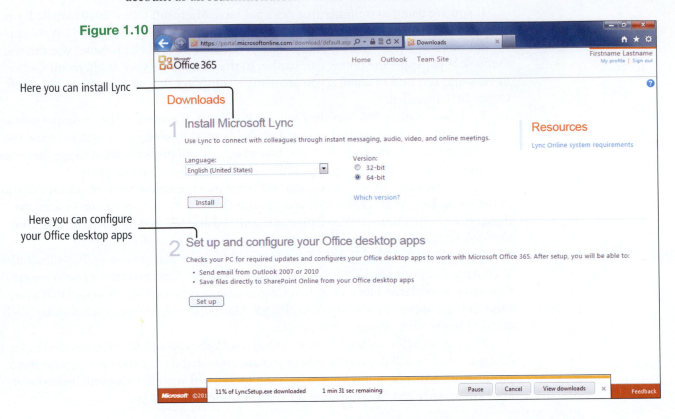

Here you can install Lync

Here you can configure your Office desktop apps

Finally, you will want to connect Outlook to your desktop, as shown in Figure 1.11, and then watch the video, which has a link as shown in Figure 1.12.

Figure 1.11

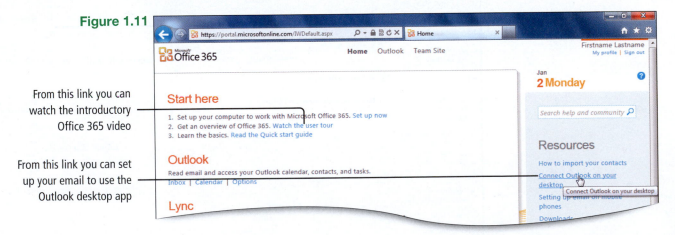

From this link you can watch the introductory Office 365 video

From this link you can set up your email to use the Outlook desktop app

Figure 1.12

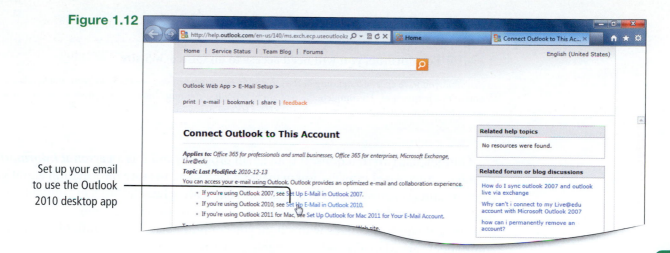

Set up your email to use the Outlook 2010 desktop app

After you have connected your email address to the Outlook desktop application, you can start Outlook, and your screen will look similar to Figure 1.13.

Figure 1.13

New Office 365 email shown in the Outlook desktop app

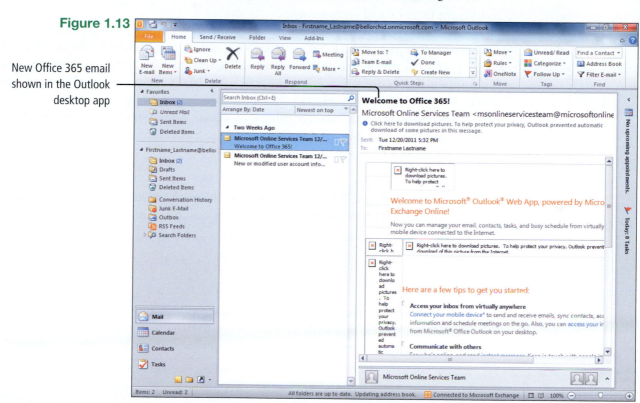

To check how well you understand the Outlook Web App and the Outlook desktop app, take a moment to answer the following questions:

1 For your personal email on your own computer, you can use Outlook as a _____ email application.

2 In Office 365, you will use Outlook to manage your Office 365 email as a Microsoft _____ account—not as a POP3 or IMAP account.

3 The programs in Microsoft Office 2010 such as Word and Excel are _____ apps.

4 Email is the most common form of communication in the _____.

5 You can switch _____ between Outlook Web App and the Outlook 2010 desktop app.

Activity 1.06 | Sending and Replying to Email

Outlook has two functions: It is an email program, and it is a *personal information manager*. A personal information manager enables you to store information about your *contacts* and also enables you keep track of your daily schedule, tasks to complete, and meetings to attend. Contacts are the names of your coworkers, customers, suppliers, friends, and family members with whom you communicate. Thus, Outlook's four major components are Mail, Calendar, Contacts, and Tasks.

Your information in Outlook is stored in folders, and there are separate folders for each of Outlook's components. For example, email is stored in a folder named *Inbox*. Outlook presents information in *views*, which are ways to look at similar information in different formats and arrangements.

To send an email message to someone, you must know the recipient's email address. There are two parts to an email address, with each part separated by the *at sign* (@). The first part is the user name of the recipient. The second part of the email address is the *domain name*. A domain name is the host name of the recipient's mail server. Recall that with Office 365, your organization has a mail server hosted by Microsoft.

You create an email message using an Outlook *form*, which is a window for displaying and collecting information. There are forms for messages, contacts, tasks, and appointments.

1 If necessary, sign *out* of your Office 365 account and close your Web browser. Close any other applications and display the Windows desktop.

2 On the taskbar, click **Start** 🪟, click **All Programs**, and then scroll down the list of programs until you see **Microsoft Lync**, **Microsoft Office**, and **Microsoft Office 365** on the list. Compare your screen with Figure 1.14.

Figure 1.14

Start menu displays
Microsoft Lync, Microsoft
Office, and Microsoft
Office 365 (your
list may vary)

3 Click **Microsoft Office**, and then, as necessary, drag the icons for **Word**, **Excel**, **PowerPoint**, **OneNote**, and **Outlook** to your taskbar.

4 On the list of programs, click the **Microsoft Office** folder to close it, and then click the **Microsoft Office 365** folder. Drag the icon for the **Microsoft Office 365 Portal** to your taskbar. Using a similar technique, open the folder for **Microsoft Lync** and then drag the **Microsoft Lync 2010** icon to your taskbar. Compare your screen with Figure 1.15.

Figure 1.15

Icon on taskbar for Lync

Icon on taskbar for
Office 365 portal

Icons on the taskbar for
Word, Excel, PowerPoint,
OneNote, and Outlook

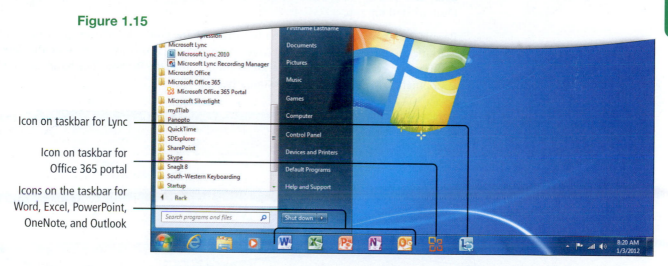

5 On the taskbar, click the **Office 365** icon to open your Web browser to the Office 365 Portal, and then sign in with your User ID and password.

6 At the top of the screen, in the heading, notice the links for *Home*, *Outlook*, and *Team Site*. Click the **Outlook** link, and then compare your screen with Figure 1.16.

Office 365 defaults to Outlook Web App unless you open the Outlook desktop application. The Outlook link at the top of your Office 365 Home page, and also the links under Outlook on the Home page, will always open Outlook Web App.

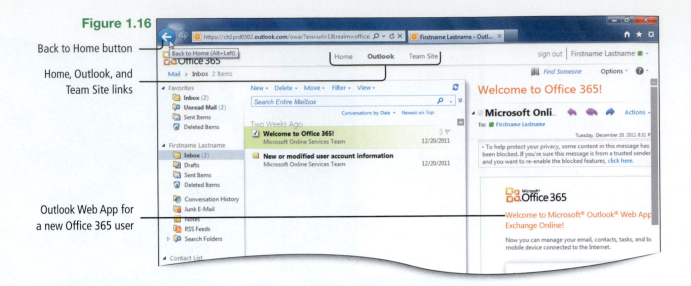

Figure 1.16

Back to Home button

Home, Outlook, and Team Site links

Outlook Web App for a new Office 365 user

7 In the upper left corner of the screen, click the **Back to Home** button ⬅ to return to your Office 365 Home page.

8 On the taskbar, click the **Outlook** icon 📧 to open your Office 365 mail in the Outlook desktop app, and then compare your screen with Figure 1.17.

Recall that Outlook Web App and the Outlook desktop app work seamlessly together, so you can work with your Outlook items—email, contacts, calendar, and tasks—from any computer with a Web browser or from any computer on which you have configured the Outlook desktop app.

Because you have set your computer to work with the Outlook desktop application, when working on the computer that you have set up, you will probably want to use the desktop application because it has more features—for example, the Ribbon. The basic features of your email, however, are arranged similarly.

Figure 1.17

Office 365 email opened in the Outlook desktop app; Ribbon displays

9 On the Ribbon, on the **Home tab**, click **New E-mail**, and then compare your screen with Figure 1.18.

The top of the form displays a Ribbon with commands organized by groups and tabs based on particular activities, such as setting message options or formatting text.

Figure 1.18

Message tab —

Ribbon —

Message area —

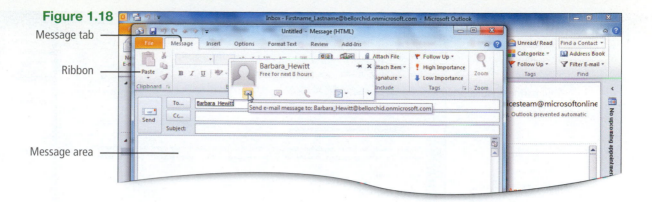

Alert! | **Does your Ribbon look different?**

The size of the Outlook window determines how much information appears with each command on the Ribbon. Users with larger screen resolutions will notice both icons and words for all commands, while those with small screens may see only the icons for certain commands.

---

10 In the **To** box, type the Office 365 email address of the classmate with whom you are partnering for this exercise. Notice that after you type the address, only the name displays. Point to your classmate's name, and then in the box that displays, click the arrow next to the small checklist as shown in Figure 1.19.

> Here you can see that the person to whom you sent the email is free for the next 8 hours (yours may differ) and that you could schedule a meeting with this person. Because you and your classmate are users of the same Exchange Online system in Office 365—you are team members in the same organization—Outlook offers you many ways to interact with each other.

Figure 1.19

Information for Barbara
Hewitt displays
(yours will differ) —

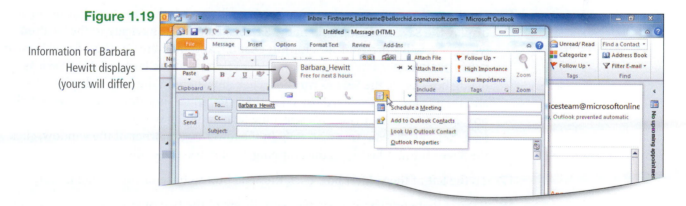

11 Click in the **Subject** box and type **Office 365 Orientation Meeting** and then press ⎄Tab. In the message box, type **Hi! Did you hear that Steven Ramos has scheduled a meeting on Friday to learn more about our new Office 365 system? I think this new system will really help our team working on the San Diego project to be more successful!**

12 Press ⎆Enter two times, and then type **See you there!** Press ⎆Enter two times, and then using your own name, type **Firstname Lastname** Compare your screen with Figure 1.20.

Figure 1.20

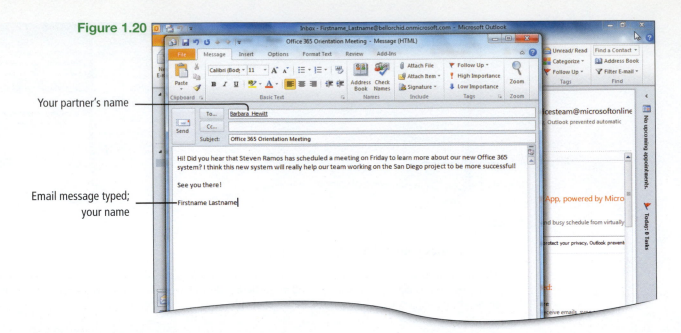

Your partner's name

Email message typed; your name

13 With your email message still displayed, display the **Start** menu 🟦, and then click **All Programs**. On the list of programs, click the **Accessories** folder to display a list of **Accessories**. Click **Snipping Tool** to display the small **Snipping Tool** window.

14 On the menu bar of the **Snipping Tool**, click the **arrow** to the right of **New**—referred to as the **New arrow**. From the displayed menu, click **Window Snip**. Then, move your mouse pointer over the email message that you typed, and notice that a *red* rectangle surrounds the window; the remainder of your screen dims.

15 With the 🖑 pointer positioned in the message, click one time.

16 On the **Snipping Tool** mark-up window's toolbar, click the **Save Snip** button 🖫 to display the **Save As** dialog box. In the **Save As** dialog box, navigate to the location where you will store your files for this chapter, and then create a new folder named **Office 365 Chapter 1** With your new folder selected, at the bottom of the **Save As** dialog box, locate the **Save as type** box, click anywhere in the box to display a list, and then from the displayed list, click **JPEG file**. At the bottom of the **Save As** dialog box, click in the **File name** box, select the text, and then using your name, type **Lastname_Firstname_1A_Email_Snip** In the lower right corner of the window, click the **Save** button. **Close** ❎ the Snipping Tool mark-up window.

17 To the left of the **Subject** box, click the **Send** button to send your email message.

18 Be sure that your partner has sent you the email the two of you just created, and then notice that in your inbox, the message displays. Click to select the message, and then on the Ribbon, click the **View tab**. In the **Layout group**, click the **Reading Pane arrow**, and then compare your screen with Figure 1.21.

Outlook's default view is to display the Reading Pane on the right. Here you have the option to have the Reading Pane on the bottom or turned off. There are other options you can set for the Reading Pane.

Figure 1.21

View tab active

Reading Pane
list displayed

Email message displays

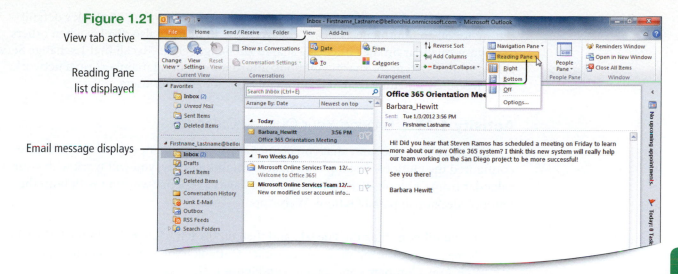

19 With the email message you received from your partner still selected and displayed in the Reading Pane, on the Ribbon, click the **Home tab**. In the **Respond group**, click **Reply**.

The message opens with space at the top for you to type a reply.

20 Type **I'm looking forward to it too!** Press [Enter] two times, and then type your name.

21 Using the technique you practiced, create a **Window Snip**, and then save the snip as a **jpeg** file in your chapter folder. Using your name, name the file **Lastname_Firstname_1A_Reply_Snip**

22 Click the **Send** button, and then leave Outlook open for the next activity.

Outlook is a rich app with many features to help you organize your communications. For an in-depth review of how to use Outlook 2010, refer to *GO! with Microsoft Outlook 2010 Comprehensive* published by Pearson or *Microsoft Outlook 2010 Inside Out* published by Microsoft Press.

Objective 3 | Share Calendars and Create Contacts

With Office 365, you set up your Calendar in Outlook—either in Outlook Web App or on the desktop app—and then you can share your calendar, add appointments and meetings, and see your calendar from anywhere that you have Internet access. Recall that Outlook Web App and the Outlook desktop app work seamlessly together. When you use the desktop app, you have some additional features that are not available in Outlook Web App, but any information you add is available in either app. You will be able to view your calendar—and use email—from your smartphone or from anywhere you have an Internet connection.

In an Office 365 environment, the most important thing to do with your calendar is to share it with others. Recall that Office 365 is specifically designed to help teams work together, and the first step to working together successfully is to share as much information as possible to facilitate good communication.

When you create an appointment in your calendar, Outlook displays one of four indicators associated with your availability for that date and time: Busy, Free, Tentative, or Out of Office. This is referred to as your *free/busy information*. Outlook's default setting for all appointments is Busy. The free/busy indicators also display when others view your calendar on the Office 365 shared Exchange server. Recall that Exchange Server is Microsoft's system for sharing Outlook information among members on a network. Your free/busy schedule is shared automatically with all other users.

Activity 1.07 | Sharing Your Outlook Calendar

For this activity, assume that you are *not* at your main computer where you have configured the Outlook desktop app. Instead, in this activity, you will work with your calendar from Outlook Web App so that you have experience working with both the Outlook desktop app and Outlook Web App.

1 On the Ribbon, click the **File tab**, and then on the left, click **Exit**. On the Office 365 Home page, at the top of the screen, click **Outlook** to open your Mail in Outlook Web App. Compare your screen with Figure 1.22.

Figure 1.22

Same email account but open in Outlook Web App

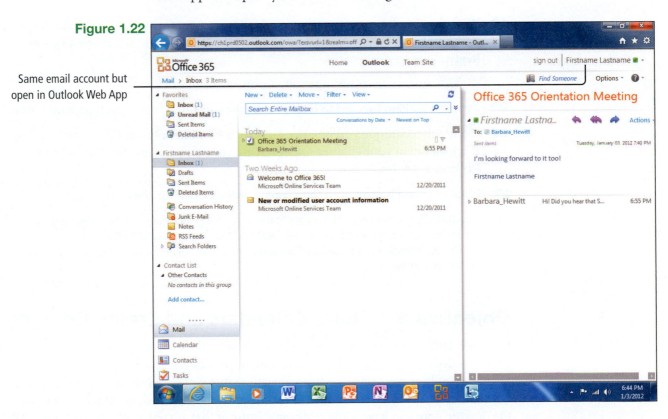

2 In the lower left, click **Calendar**, and then above the calendar, click **Share**. Compare your screen with Figure 1.23.

> In an Exchange Online environment, you can share your calendar with other Exchange Online users in your organization. Additionally, you can publish your calendar to the Internet and invite other people to access it. For example, you might want to share your calendar with a customer or client while working on an important project, and then discontinue sharing when the project is complete.
>
> You can also send your calendar to someone by email, save your calendar as a Web page, and then send it or post your calendar to a Web server.

Figure 1.23

Share button

Calendar active

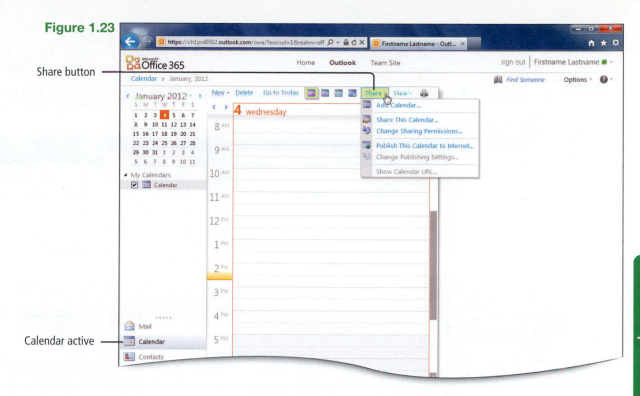

3 On the list, click **Share This Calendar**, and then in the **Sharing Invitation**, in the **To** box, type the Office 365 email address of the classmate with whom you are partnering for this project. In the **Share** area, click **All information**, and then select the **I want to request permission to view the recipient's Calendar folder** checkbox.

4 Press Tab one time to move to the message area, and then type **While we are working together on the San Diego project, let's share our calendar information.** Compare your screen with Figure 1.24.

There are numerous permission levels you can set when sharing your calendar with others, and you may want to investigate these in detail before actually sharing a calendar.

Figure 1.24

Click here to send the message

Calendar sharing invitation filled in

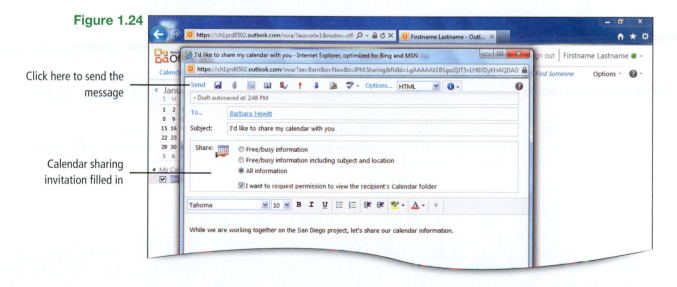

5 In the upper left corner, click **Send**.

When you receive the email from your partner, your system may play a short, soft sound and briefly display the person's name in a small box in the upper portion of the screen.

6 In the lower left corner, click **Mail** to return to your Mail folder, and then click the email message from your partner. Compare your screen with Figure 1.25.

Figure 1.25

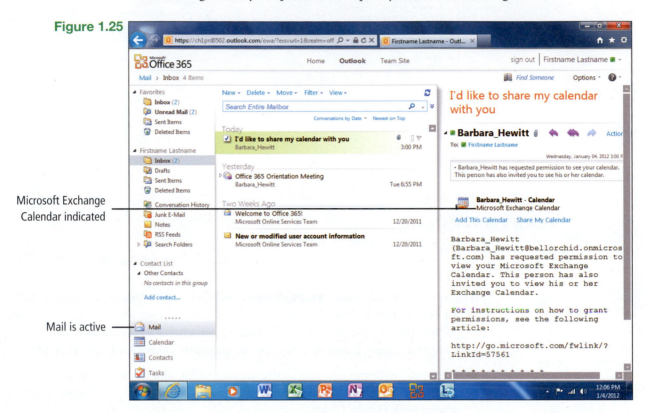

Microsoft Exchange
Calendar indicated

Mail is active

7 Using the technique you have practiced, create a **Window Snip**, and then save the snip as a **jpeg** file in your chapter folder. Using your name, name the file **Lastname_ Firstname_1A_Calendar_Snip** and then **Close** the Snipping Tool mark-up window.

Activity 1.08 | Creating Outlook Contacts

Your Contacts folder stores all the details about your contacts—the people, businesses, and organizations that you communicate with. After a contact is added to your folder, you can add details about and take actions on that contact. For example, you can associate a contact with a document, connect a contact to a Web site, schedule meetings with the contact, or assign a task to a contact—assuming that the appropriate Outlook permissions are in place.

1 In the lower left, click **Contacts** to open your Contacts folder. In the upper portion of the screen, click **New**, and then add the following contact—if no information is provided, leave the field empty:

First name	**Steven**
Middle name	
Last name	**Ramos**
File as	**Last, First**
Job title	**IT Specialist**
Office	**B20-2**
Department	**Information Technology**
Company	**Bell Orchid Hotels**
Manager	**Clint Williams**
Assistant	**Jen Jacobson**
Business phone	**617-555-0488**
Home phone	
Mobile phone	**617-555-0923**
Assistant	
E-mail	**Steven_Ramos@bellorchid.onmicrosoft.com**

2 In the upper left corner, click **Save and Close**, and then compare your screen with Figure 1.26.

By storing contact information in Office 365, your contacts are available to you from anywhere you have an Internet connection, including on your mobile phone and tablet.

Figure 1.26

New contact added

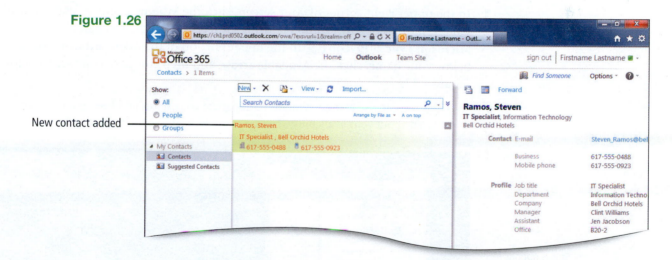

3 Using the technique you have practiced, create a **Window Snip**, and then save the snip as a **jpeg** file in your chapter folder. Using your name, name the file **Lastname_Firstname_1A_Contact_Snip** and then **Close** [×] the Snipping Tool mark-up window.

4 At the top of your screen, click **Home** to return to the Office 365 Home page.

Objective 4 | Communicate with Lync Online

In Office 365, Lync provides an integrated communications package with which you identify and list all of your contacts, arrange contacts into groups, and then display your frequent contacts at the top of the list. Then, you can send an instant message to one or more of your contacts or groups, launch an audio or video call to selected contacts, share the desktop of a colleague across the room or across the country, or take control of another person's desktop to help solve problems.

Activity 1.09 | Working with Contacts in Lync

The Bell Orchid Hotels group has key employees in offices throughout the country, and these individuals are frequently on the road. To facilitate rapid, accurate, secure communication between these employees, each computer must be set up to perform all of the necessary communication tasks. When an employee is added to the Bell Orchid Office 365 team, the Lync Setup program must be run on his or her computer, as described in Activity 1.05.

Steven Ramos has just set up his Lync client and would like to add contacts from both inside and outside the company. This will enable him to communicate with his contacts quickly and efficiently and will enable him to see who is available at any given time. It will also enable him to display his own status. The Microsoft Lync window on your computer is referred to as the *Lync client*.

> **Alert!** | Be sure that the classmate with whom you are partnering is online and ready to work with you to complete the remainder of this project. Additionally, ask one other classmate to be online so that you can practice a three-way IM conversation.

1 In the upper right corner of your screen, click the **Minimize** button to display your Windows desktop without closing Office 365. On the taskbar, click the **Microsoft Lync 2010** icon. In the upper portion of the **Microsoft Lync** window, below your name, click the **Available arrow**, and then compare your screen with Figure 1.27.

Here you can use various symbols to designate your status and keep your colleagues advised about your availability. Here you can also sign out of or exit Lync.

Figure 1.27

Status options in Lync window

2 On the list, click **Available**. Point to and then click anywhere in the text *Set your location*, and then type **San Bernardino office**

3 Click in the **Find a contact** box, and then type the first few letters of the user ID of your partner. Compare your screen with Figure 1.28.

> When you type the initial letters of the user ID of anyone in your Office 365 organization, that person's name will display in the list of contacts.

Figure 1.28

Your name (yours will vary)
Your status
Your location
Initial letters of colleague's user ID (yours will vary)
Colleague's user ID

4 Point to the colleague's name to display a + sign to its right, and then notice the ScreenTip *Add to Contacts*. Click the **Add to Contacts arrow**, and then click **Pin to Frequent Contacts**. Compare your screen with Figure 1.29.

> When you add someone to your contact list, he or she is notified and can then click a checkbox to add *your* name to his or her contact list. By adding individuals to your Frequent Contacts in Lync, you can to see their status and communicate with them quickly.

Figure 1.29

Add to Contacts button
Click here to add person to Frequent Contacts

5 Use the technique you practiced in steps 3 and 4 to add a second name to your list of **Frequent Contacts**.

6 Click in the **Find a contact** box, and then type the full e-mail address of someone *not* in your organization—for example, your own personal email address. Point to the e-mail address, click the **Add to Contacts arrow,** and then click **All Contacts**.

> If you have business contacts that you need to contact regularly, but who are not members of your Office 365 group, you can add them to your Lync client contact list by typing the entire e-mail address.

7 Start the **Snipping Tool**, create a **Window Snip**, and then save the snip as a **jpeg** file in your chapter folder. Using your name, name the file **Lastname_Firstname_1A_Lync_Snip** and then **Close** ![close button] the Snipping Tool mark-up window.

Activity 1.10 | Sending Instant Messages with Lync

When you want to ask a quick question or pass along information to a colleague, you can use Lync instant messaging. Recall that Lync provides instant messaging in a secure environment.

1 Click the name of the first person in your **Frequent Contacts** list—be sure you point to the person's name.

To the right, a small menu displays with icons representing different ways you can contact this person—by email, by instant message, by Lync call, and so on.

2 In the small menu box, click the icon with the ScreenTip *View more options for interacting with this person*, and then compare your screen with Figure 1.30.

Figure 1.30

View more options for interacting with the person arrow

Second name added to Frequent Contacts

Contact added from outside your organization

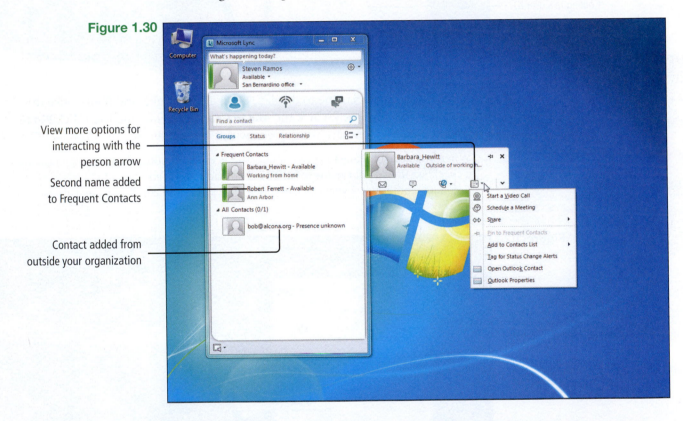

3 In your **Frequent Contacts** list, click the name of the classmate with whom you are partnering on this project, and then in the box that displays, click the **Send an instant message** icon. Type **Have you seen the new marketing presentation yet?** and then press ⏎.

4 Ask your partner to type **Yes. I saw it yesterday. It needs work.** and then press ⏎. Compare your screen with Figure 1.31.

Figure 1.31

Type of conversation is highlighted

Instant message from you

Instant message response from your colleague

5 On the command bar, click the **People Options** button ![People Options icon], and then click **Invite by Name or Phone Number**. From the list of contacts, select another classmate who is online, and then click **OK**.

6 Type the person's first name and a comma, type **have you got a second?** and then press ⏎. Notice that the number of participants displays in the title bar of the dialog box, and the conversation is listed as a *Group Conversation*, as shown in Figure 1.32.

Figure 1.32

Number of participants in conversation

List as a Group Conversation

People Options button

Another contact added to conversation

7 **Close** ![Close button] the **Group Conversation** window.

Activity 1.11 | Launching a Video Call with Lync

If your computer is set up for sound and video, the Lync client enables you to participate in video calls. Video calls are more personal than instant messaging, and communicating with video usually results in fewer miscommunications and misunderstandings.

1 Be sure your partner is online with proper equipment—you can both be in the same room if you want.

2 On your **Frequent Contacts** list, *double-click* your partner's name—this is another method to display contact methods. In the command bar, click **Video** to display a message on your partner's screen.

3 Have your partner click *your* name in the message box, click the **Video arrow**, and then click **Start My Video**.

> You and your partner should be able to see and hear each other. You may have to adjust the volume control on each computer to hear properly—each computer's equipment is different.

4 In your video presentation window, point to your partner's name. Click the **View more options for calling this person arrow** ▣ ▾, and then click **Type a conversation subject**. Type **Marketing presentation** and then press (Enter).

> The conversation subject displays in the conversation window.

5 Adjust your camera angles and distances so that you are both easy to see in the **Marketing presentation** window. Compare your screen with Figure 1.33.

Figure 1.33

Conversation subject displays in title bar

Two people with status listed as In a call

Your colleague's picture in video window (yours will vary)

Your picture in video window (yours will vary)

Robert Ferrett

6 Start the **Snipping Tool**, create a **Full-screen Snip**, and then save the snip as a **jpeg** file in your chapter folder. Using your own name, name the file **Lastname_Firstname_1A_Video_Snip** and then **Close** ▣✖ the Snipping Tool mark-up window.

7 In the **Marketing presentation** window, click the **Close** ▣✖ button to end the call. When prompted, click **OK**.

Activity 1.12 | Controlling Another Computer's Desktop

When you have a computer problem or want assistance with an ongoing project, it is often helpful to have a colleague look at your computer screen. If that colleague is in another location, Lync in Office 365 enables you to share your desktop with—and even give control of your desktop to—a teammate. In this activity, Barbara gives control of her desktop to Steven so that he can assist her with a PowerPoint presentation she is creating.

1 Have your partner navigate to the location where the student files for this textbook are stored, and then locate and open **o01A_Marketing_Presentation**—a PowerPoint presentation.

2 In his or her Microsoft Lync window, have your partner point to your name, click the **Share button arrow**, point to **Share**, and then click **Desktop**. Compare your screen with Figure 1.34.

Your name displays in a Conversation window, and a message box notifies you that if you choose to share your desktop, all conversation participants will be able to see everything on your screen. This would include all icons on your taskbar and any instant messages that might pop up during the conversation.

Figure 1.34

Your name displays in a conversation window (yours will vary)

Robert Ferrett

3 Have your partner click **OK**. On your screen, click **Join** to join the conversation and share the screen. If necessary, **Maximize** the Lync window. On the line between the left and right portions of the screen, point to the **Hide conversation** button, and then compare your screen with 1.35.

The Conversation pane displays on the left, and the shared screen displays on the right. If you want to conduct this conversation as a video call, each participant needs to click the Video arrow, and then click Add Video. If you do not plan to open a video call, it is a good idea to close the Conversation pane.

Figure 1.35

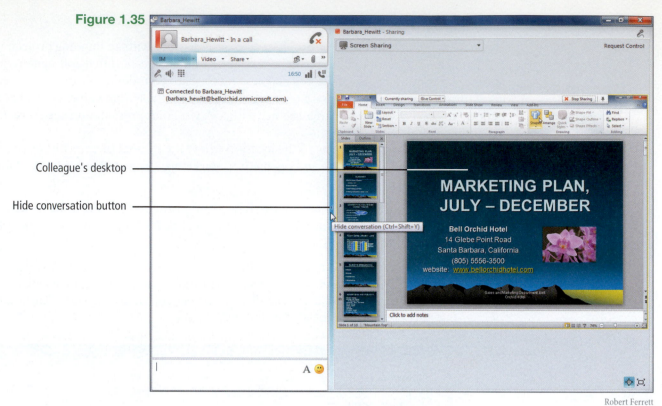

Colleague's desktop

Hide conversation button

Robert Ferrett

4 Click the **Hide conversation** button, and notice that the shared desktop is much larger and easier to read.

5 At the top of the shared screen, have your partner click the **Give Control** button, and then click your name.

> To take back control of the screen, your partner can press Ctrl + Alt + Spacebar.

6 In the message box, have your partner click **OK** to turn over control of the screen to you. Move your pointer to the left side of the PowerPoint window and click the second thumbnail—the **SUMMARY** slide.

7 On the slide, in the last bullet point, select the text *January - June*, and then type **First Six Months** Compare your screen with Figure 1.36.

> To take back control of the screen, your partner must press Ctrl + Alt + Spacebar. The changes display on your screen *and* on the shared screen.

Figure 1.36

Person whose desktop is shared

Indicates you are in control of desktop

Click here to release control

Second slide selected

Text replaced on colleague's desktop

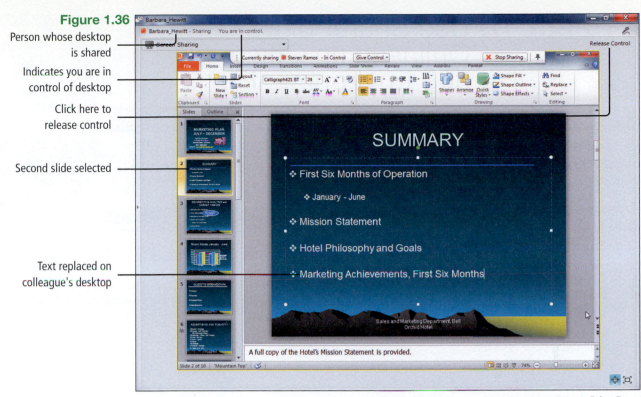

Robert Ferrett

8   In the upper right corner of your screen, click the **Release Control** button. Notice that the *Release Control* button changes to a *Request Control* button in case you would like to take over control of the shared screen again.

9   **Close**  the conversation on your screen, and then, in the **Microsoft Lync** window, just below your name, click the **Available arrow**, and then click **Exit**. Have your partner close the PowerPoint presentation without saving the changes, and then **Exit** Microsoft Lync.

10   On the taskbar, click the **Internet Explorer** button 🅮 to redisplay your Office 365 Home page, and then, in the upper right corner, click **Sign out**.

11   Submit the six snip files that you created in this project to your instructor as directed.

End   You have completed Project 1A ————————————————

Project 1B Use SharePoint Online in an Office 365 Environment

Project Activities

In Activities 1.13 through 1.21, you will use SharePoint Online to create and add content to a team site, share team knowledge, and survey team members. As you work, you will capture six screens that will look similar to Figure 1.37.

Project Files

For Project 1B, you will need the following files:

o01B_Curtis_Letter
o01B_Letter
o01B_Marketing
o01B_Orchid
o01B_Room_Sales

You will save your files as:

Lastname_Firstname_1B_Welcome_Snip
Lastname_Firstname_1B_Calendar_Snip
Lastname_Firstname_1B_Library_Snip
Lastname_Firstname_1B_Discussion_Snip
Lastname_Firstname_1B_Wiki_Snip
Lastname_Firstname_1B_Survey_Snip

Project Results

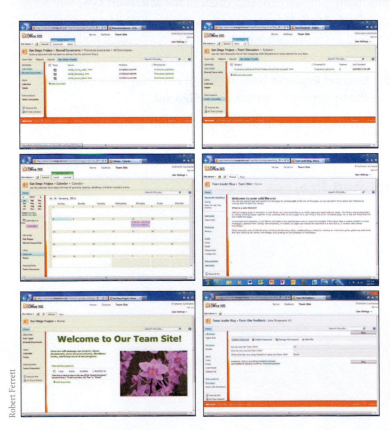

Robert Ferrett

Figure 1.37

Objective 5 | Create a Team Site

Think about a project that you have worked on with others. Maybe it was a class project to gather information and then make a class presentation, or maybe it was a club project to plan an event. You probably had a central place—a room in your Student Center or space in someone's home—where you kept all the information related to the project. A portable table and folding chairs became the meeting place; maybe there was a bulletin board to post notices and a file cabinet with associated documents. Perhaps there was a computer and a telephone. If you have work experience, you have probably seen conference rooms where similar activities take place.

Activity 1.13 | Creating a Team Site

An Office 365 team site is a Web site—accessible only to those with permission—where a team can organize, author, and share information, and that includes a *document library*, and *lists* for managing announcements, calendar items, tasks, and discussions. A document library is a storage container—similar to a Windows folder—but with additional functionality, such as version tracking, and which provides for central storage as opposed to storage on a local hard drive. A list is a collection of like items, such as contact information or inventory items.

Think of your Office 365 team site as a virtual space where you and your teammates can meet and share what you have been working on. In this virtual office space, you will be able to find the documents and information you need, communicate with teammates, post announcements and progress reports, and manage and assign all the tasks related to the project.

Office 365 comes with a Team Site under which you can create additional sites—referred to as *subsites*—to organize content. A subsite can have additional subsites under it. In this manner, you create a hierarchical *site collection*—a group of Web sites within your Office 365 installation that has the same owner and shares administrative settings such as permissions.

An organization can decide on whatever site structure they need. For example, you might create subsites for departments or for projects or for locations. For Bell Orchid Hotels, a site collection might look like the one shown in Figure 1.38, which has a subsite for projects involving new hotels.

Figure 1.38

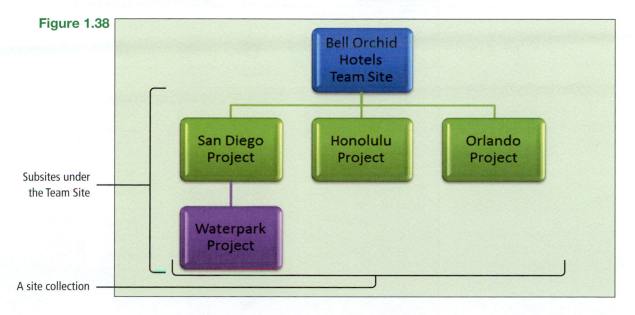

Your Office 365 Administrator typically designs and controls the top-level Team Site—the site to which you link from the top of your home page. From the top-level Team Site, you can link to other subsites to which you have been given access, or you can design and control a subsite to which you have been given full permissions; that is, you are the site *owner*. To create a subsite under the top-level Team Site, your Office 365 Administrator will sign on as the Admin, as shown in Figure 1.39.

Figure 1.39

When signed in as Admin, Admin link displays

Signed in as Admin

Under Team sites and documents, Admin activates Add sites and templates

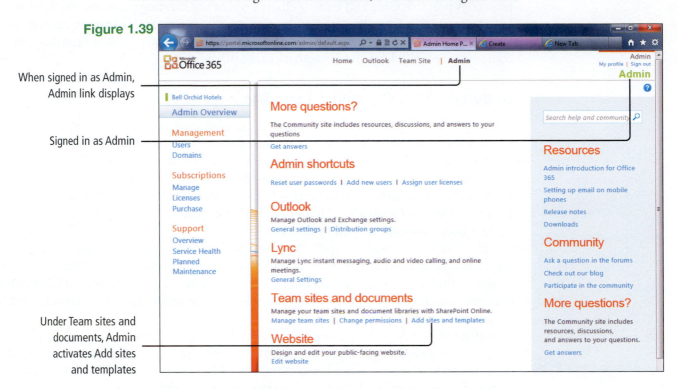

Then the Admin displays the Create page, as shown in Figure 1.40. Here, your Admin can select a Blank Site or select from among many predesigned templates for a subsites.

Figure 1.40

Create tab

Types of sites

Basic Meeting Workspace

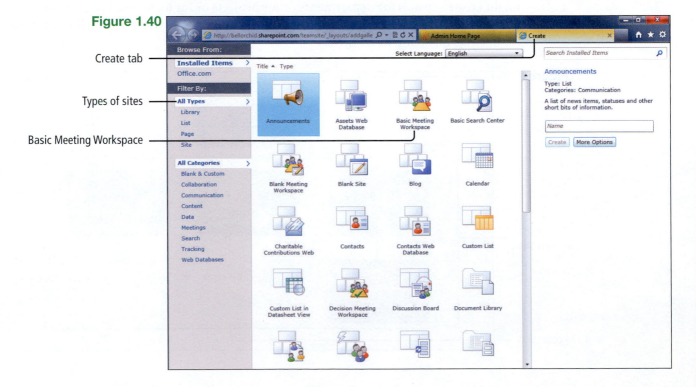

Having different types of site templates is useful because not every subsite needs every SharePoint capability. For example, as shown in Figure 1.40, under All Categories, there are templates for Collaboration sites, Meetings sites, and so on.

As shown in Figure 1.41, there are predesigned templates for different types of meeting sites—one of the site categories. For example, you could set up a *Basic Meeting Workspace*, which is a site to plan, organize, and capture the results of a meeting; it provides lists for managing the agenda, meeting attendees, and documents.

Figure 1.41

Types of Meeting sites

Meetings category selected

As shown in Figure 1.42, for the Bell Orchid Hotels employees that are working on the San Diego project, the Admin will create a Collaboration site using the Team Site template and name the site *San Diego*.

Figure 1.42

Type of site is Team Site

Name assigned to site

Category of site is Collaboration

Text with no spaces to indicate the ending of site's URL

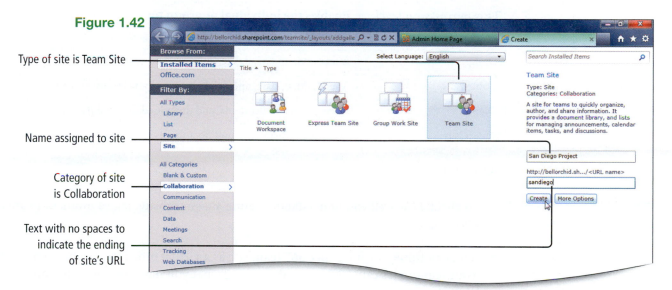

After a subsite is created, a screen similar to Figure 1.43 displays, at which point the Admin can assign permissions to the San Diego team members so that they can design and contribute to—use—their subsite.

Figure 1.43

New site created for the
San Diego Project

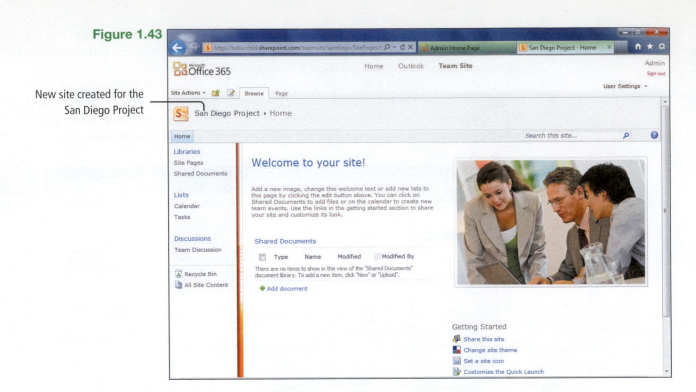

The levels of permission in SharePoint are shown in the table in Figure 1.44.

Permission Levels in Office 365	
This permission level:	**Enables the individual or group to:**
Full Control	Have full control of all content, design, and permissions.
Design	View, add, update, delete, approve, and customize content.
Contribute	View, add, update, and delete list items and documents.
Read	View pages and list items, and download documents.
View Only	View pages, list items, and documents.

Figure 1.44

To check how well you understand creating a team subsite, take a moment to answer the following questions:

1 You can think of your Office 365 team site as a virtual office space where you and your teammates can _____ and _____ what you have been working on.

2 The site to which you link when you click Team Site at the top of your Office 365 Home page is referred to as the _____ Team Site.

3 You can design and control a subsite to which you have been given full permissions, meaning you are the site _____.

4 There are many different templates for subsites because not every subsite needs every SharePoint _____.

5 After a subsite is created by the Office 365 Administrator, he or she will assign _____ so that team members can design and use their subsite.

More Knowledge | **SharePoint Online Also Includes a Public Web Site**

Your Office 365 SharePoint Online installation has two sites when you begin: The Team Site for internal use and a public Web site that serves as your organization's Web presence. If you would like to view some examples of public Web sites hosted on an Office SharePoint Server, go to http://www.wssdemo.com/pages/websites.aspx.

Activity 1.14 | Modifying Your Site's Home Page

A team site can be simple or complex in design. Recall that the team site is accessible from anywhere and any device that can connect to the Internet with a browser. It is a Web site that only you and your team members can access.

To make your site distinctive for your team, you can begin by changing the site theme and deciding on the text layout of your page.

Alert! | **Ask your instructor for access to your assigned subsite.**

You are ready to work with an Office 365 subsite to which you have full permissions. As the Office 365 Administrator, your instructor can create a team site for you to work with in this project.

---

1 Sign in to your Office 365 account, and at the top of the page, click the **Team Site** link. Take a moment to study the navigation tools described in the table in Figure 1.45, and then compare your screen with Figure 1.46.

Navigation Tools in a SharePoint Site

Tool	Description
Top link bar	A series of links at the top of the screen separated by ▶ symbols to indicate a path from the current site to the sites that are one level below the current site in the hierarchy; each link is an active control that you can click to move directly to the location.
Quick Launch	A column of links on the left side of a SharePoint site with which you can navigate to important content in the current site; for example lists and libraries.
Navigate Up button	An icon above the top link bar that displays where you are in the site hierarchy; by expanding the list with this button, you can jump quickly to another location. Use the Navigate Up button to navigate back to pages that are closer in hierarchy to the Home page.
Ribbon	The area at the top of the screen that contains tabs to expose the Ribbon commands, similar to the Ribbon in Microsoft Office 2010 applications.
Navigation bar	Tabs above the Quick Launch that link to subsites and selected pages.

Figure 1.45

Figure 1.46

Added San Diego Project
Team Site (yours may
differ depending on the
name your instructor
chooses for the site)
available from both the
Quick Launch and the
navigation bar

2 On the **navigation bar** or on the **Quick Launch**, click the name of the site your
instructor has assigned to you—in this example the site is *San Diego Project*.

3 In the lower right portion of the screen, click **Change site theme**, and then on the right,
click **Cay**. In the lower right corner, click **Apply**, and then compare your screen with
Figure 1.47.

> The Site Settings screen displays with the new colors. From this screen, you can manage
> the site.

Figure 1.47

Site Settings screen
displays

New theme applied

4 On the **navigation bar**, click the name of your site to navigate back to the Home page,
and then compare your screen with Figure 1.48.

Figure 1.48

Browse tab ——

Edit button ——

Home page for your
site; new colors display ——

5 On the Ribbon, to the left of the **Browse tab**, click the **Edit** button ▨ to add the **Editing Tools** to the Ribbon. Click the **Format Text tab**, and then in the **Layout group**, click the **Text Layout** button. On the list, click **Two columns with header**.

6 Click in the header area to display the blinking insertion point, and then type **Welcome to Our Team Site!** Select the text you just typed, and then in the **Font group**, change the **Font Size** to **36pt**, apply **Bold**, and change the **Font Color** to **Dark Green, Accent 6 Darkest**—in the last column the last color. In the **Paragraph group**, **Center** the text.

7 To the left of the picture, select all of the text and press ⌫Delete. Press ⌫Backspace as many times as necessary to position the insertion point at the top of the box, and then type **Here we will manage our project, share documents, post announcements, distribute tasks, and keep track of our progress.** Select the text you just typed and change the **Font Color** to **Dark Green, Accent 6 Darkest**, change the **Font Size** to **10pt**, and apply **Bold**.

8 On the right, click the picture to select it, and then press ⌫Delete. On the Ribbon, click the **Insert tab**, and then in the **Media group**, click the **Picture** button. In the **Select Picture** dialog box, click **Browse**, navigate to the student files that accompany this text, click **o01B_Orchid**, and then click **Open**. Click **OK**, and then click **Save**.

9 On the Ribbon, on the **Design tab**, change the **Horizontal Size** to **400 px**. On the Ribbon, click the **Save & Close** button ▨ to save the changes you have made to your site. Compare your screen with Figure 1.49.

Figure 1.49

Path to San Diego Project Home

Text added

Picture changed

Robert Ferrett

10 Display the **Start** menu 🪟, and then click **All Programs**. On the list of programs, click the **Accessories** folder to display a list of **Accessories**. Click **Snipping Tool** to display the small **Snipping Tool** window.

11 On the menu bar of the **Snipping Tool**, click the **arrow** to the right of **New**—referred to as the **New arrow**. From the displayed menu, click **Window Snip**. Then, move your mouse pointer anywhere over the screen, and notice that a *red* rectangle surrounds the window; the remainder of your screen dims.

12 With the 👆 pointer positioned on the Home page, click the left mouse button one time.

13 On the **Snipping Tool** mark-up window's toolbar, click the **Save Snip** button 💾 to display the **Save As** dialog box. In the **Save As** dialog box, navigate to your **Office 365 Chapter 1** folder. With your folder selected, at the bottom of the **Save As** dialog box, locate the **Save as type** box, click anywhere in the box to display a list, and then from the displayed list, click **JPEG file**. At the bottom of the **Save As** dialog box, click in the **File name** box, select the text, and then using your name, type **Lastname_Firstname_1B_Welcome_Snip** In the lower right corner of the window, click the **Save** button. **Close** ❎ the Snipping Tool mark-up window.

Objective 6 | Add Content to a Team Site

Activity 1.15 | Adding and Editing Calendar Events

A SharePoint calendar that all team members can access is useful to keep track of important milestones, project meetings, and other events. A site can have more than one calendar. In this activity, you will add and edit events in a calendar.

1 On the **Quick Launch**, click **Calendar**, and then compare your screen with Figure 1.50.

The Calendar displays, and on the Ribbon, Calendar Tools are active.

Figure 1.50

Calendar Tools
active on the Ribbon

Calendar (your dates
will differ)

Calendar active

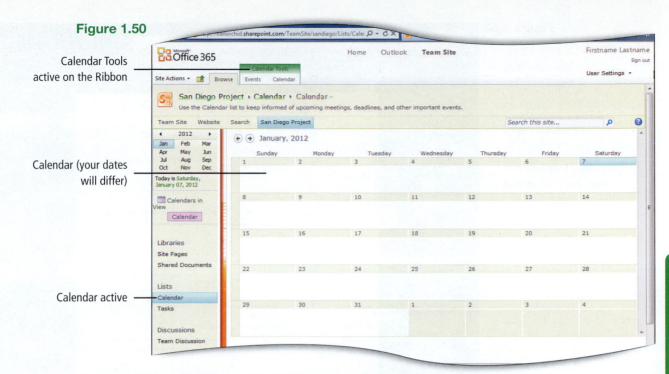

2 On the Ribbon, click the **Calendar tab**, and then, in the **Scope group**, click the **Week** button. Compare your screen with Figure 1.51.

The calendar displays in the weekly view.

Figure 1.51

Week button active
in the Scope group

Calendar displays in
Week view

3 On the Ribbon, click the **Events tab**, and then in the **New group**, click the upper portion of the **New Event** button. In the **Calendar – New Item** dialog box, with the insertion point blinking in the **Title** box, type **Planning Meeting**

4 In the **Location** box, type **Steve Ramos' Office** In the **Start Time** box, leave the current date and select **9AM** as the start time. In the **End Time** box, leave the current date and select **10AM** as the end time. In the **Description** box, type **Please review the attached document before the meeting.** Compare your screen with Figure 1.52.

Figure 1.52

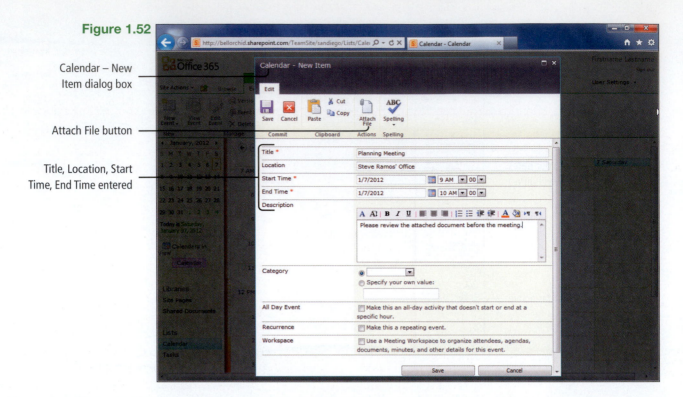

Calendar – New
Item dialog box

Attach File button

Title, Location, Start
Time, End Time entered

5 On the **Edit tab**, in the **Actions group**, click the **Attach File** button. Click the **Browse** button, navigate to the location where the student files for this textbook are stored, select **o01B_Letter**, and then click **Open**. Click **OK**.

6 On the **Edit tab**, in the **Spelling group**, click the upper portion of the **Spelling** button. Make corrections until *No spelling errors found displays* in the **Spell check** dialog box, and then click **OK**. On the **Edit tab**, in the **Commit group**, click the **Save** button. Compare your screen with Figure 1.53.

The event is saved, and the Planning Meeting in Steve Ramos' office displays on the calendar.

Figure 1.53

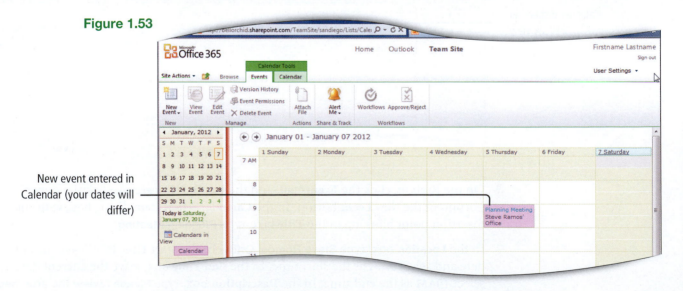

New event entered in
Calendar (your dates will
differ)

7 On the calendar, point to the text *Planning Meeting* to display the 🖑 pointer, and then click to display the details of the calendar event. Notice that you can see the name of the attachment. Click **Close** to close the Calendar dialog box.

8 Point to the lower portion of the **Planning Meeting** event to display the ▷ pointer, and then drag the item to a different day and time of your choice. Then double-click the meeting to view the meeting details again. Notice that the new date and times display.

9 Using the technique you practiced, create a **Window Snip**, click to capture the snip, and then save the snip as a **jpeg** file in your chapter folder. Using your own name, name the file **Firstname_Lastname_1B_Calendar_Snip**

10 Click **Close** to close the dialog box. On the **Quick Launch**, under **Lists**, click **Calendar**, and then, on the **top link bar**, click the name of your site to return to the site's home page.

Activity 1.16 | Creating Folders and Uploading Documents in a Document Library

Recall that in SharePoint, a document library is similar to a Windows folder, but includes additional functionality, such as version tracking, and provides for central storage as opposed to storage on a local hard drive. Additionally, a SharePoint document library is stored in a database rather than a file system, thus enabling more sophisticated handling of documents.

A library can store documents, spreadsheets, pictures, and many additional file types. The files can be accessed and modified by others who have permissions.

1 On the **Quick Launch**, click **Libraries**, and then under **Document Libraries**, click **Shared Documents**. Compare your screen with Figure 1.54.

On the Ribbon, the Library Tools are active.

Figure 1.54

Library Tools active on the Ribbon

Top link bar indicates path to Shared Documents

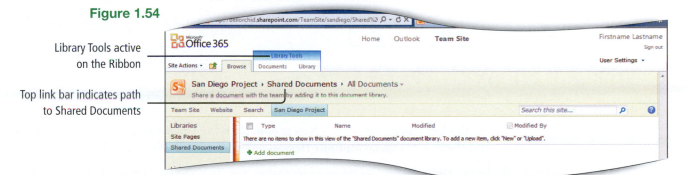

2 On the Ribbon, click the **Documents tab**, and then in the **New group**, click the **New Folder** button. In the **Name** box, using your own name, type **Firstname_Lastname** and then click **Save**. Compare your screen with Figure 1.55.

Figure 1.55

New Folder button

New folder added (yours should display your own name)

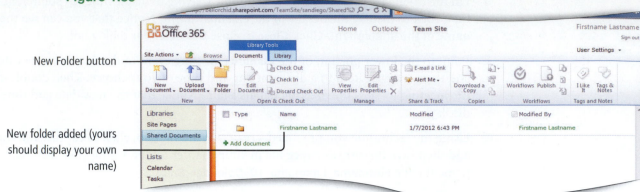

3 Double-click the name of your new folder to open it, and then on the **Documents tab**, in the **New group**, click the upper portion of the **Upload Document** button. If necessary, click the yellow warning bar at the top or bottom of your screen, click Run Add-on, and then click Run—or click Allow; click the Upload Document button again.

4 With the insertion point blinking in the **Name** box, click the **Browse** button, and then navigate to the location where the student files for this textbook are stored. Select the Excel file **o01B_Room_Sales**, click **Open**, and then click **OK**. Compare your screen with Figure 1.56.

Figure 1.56

Excel file stored in the folder

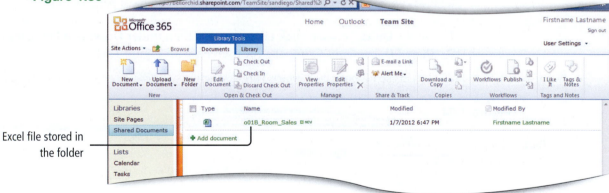

5 On the **Documents tab**, in the **New group**, click the **Upload Document button arrow**, and then click **Upload Multiple Documents**.

6 In the **Upload Multiple Documents** dialog box, in the shaded box, click **Browse for files instead**, and then navigate to the location where your student files are stored. While holding down Ctrl, click the PowerPoint file **o01B_Marketing** and the Word file **o01B_Curtis_Letter.docx**. Click **Open**, click **OK**, and then click **Done**. Compare your screen with Figure 1.57.

Figure 1.57

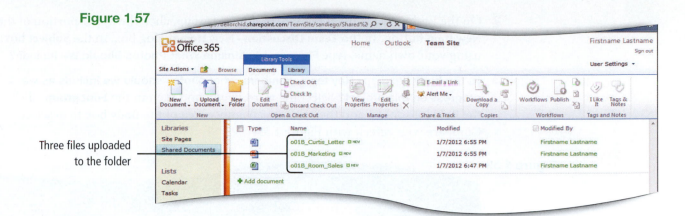

Three files uploaded
to the folder

7 Using the technique you practiced, create a **Window Snip**, click to capture the snip, and then save the snip as a **jpeg** file in your chapter folder. Using your own name, name the file **Lastname_Firstname_1B_Library_Snip**

Objective 7 | Share Team Knowledge

You have seen how a team can, by working in the cloud, share a calendar and share documents. You do not have to wonder on whose hard drive a specific file is located, because all the documents are stored in the cloud—on your team site. By posting the calendar, everyone on the team can see when meetings and events will take place. In the following activities, you will see how team members can share their knowledge with each other.

Activity 1.17 | Creating a Team Discussion

1 On the **Quick Launch**, click **Discussions**. Under **Discussion Boards**, click **Team Discussion**. Compare your screen with Figure 1.58.

The List Tools are active on the Ribbon.

Figure 1.58

List Tools active
on the Ribbon

Top link bar
indicates path

No new discussion items
currently posted

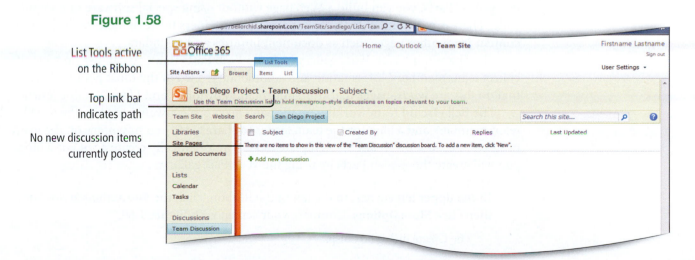

2 On the Ribbon, click the **Items tab**. In the **New group**, click the upper portion of the **New Item** button. In the **Team Discussion - New Item** dialog box, in the **Subject** box, using your own name, type **Firstname Lastname What Photos Should We Include?**

3 In the **Body** box, type **Hey team members, what photos should we include as we progress on this project?** Select the word *photos* and then in the **Font group**, click the **Bold** button $\boxed{B}$, and then click in an empty area of the **Body** box to deselect. Compare your screen with Figure 1.59.

Figure 1.59

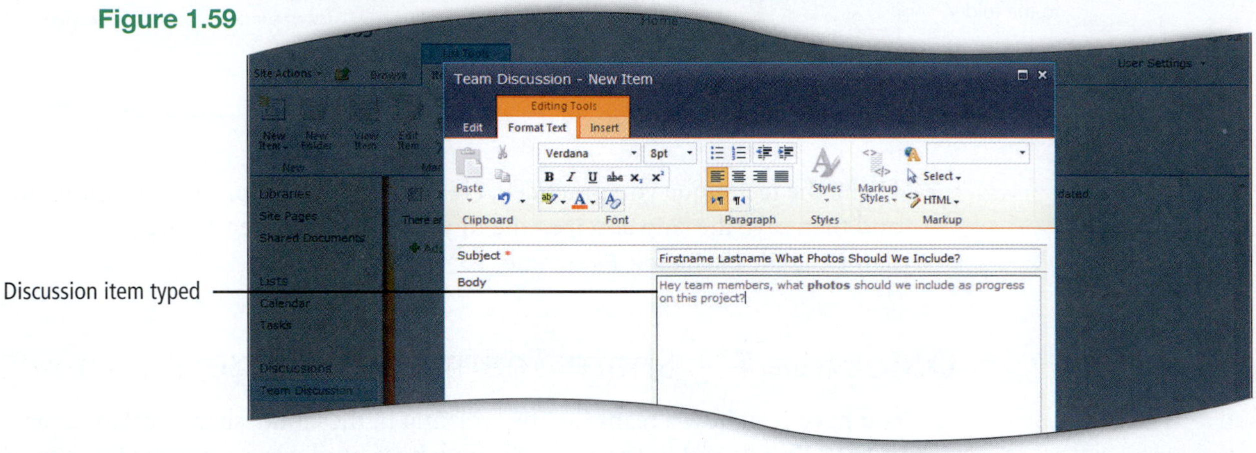

Discussion item typed

4 Click **Save**. Notice that others in your class might have also posted to this Discussion Board.

5 Using the technique you have practiced, create a **Window Snip**, click to capture the snip, and then save the snip as a **jpeg** file in your chapter folder. Using your own name, name the file **Lastname_Firstname_1B_Discussion_Snip**

Activity 1.18 | Creating a Blog and a Wiki

A *Web Part*—a mini-application or module that displays information on a page or performs a special function—is the basic building block of a SharePoint Online site. By using Web Parts, you can build a Web page without using special software or computer code. There are various Web Parts that serve as containers for text, pictures, links, and content from other pages such as document libraries and calendars.

The SharePoint Web Parts gallery includes Web Parts that you can use on your site to collect team members' information and commentary. Two of the most popular Web Parts that do this are *wikis*–pages that store information by topic, and *blogs*—online journals.

The Bell Orchid team working on the San Diego project wants a wiki to be used by all team members and a blog for the team leader to share a daily commentary on the team's progress. Because the Team Site template did not automatically create a wiki or a blog, you will create these Web Parts by using the Web Part gallery.

1 In the upper left corner, to the left of the Ribbon, click the **Site Actions arrow**, and then click **More Options**. Compare your screen with Figure 1.60.

The Create dialog box displays.

Figure 1.60

Dialog box to create item

2 Scroll down as necessary, and then click **Blog**. In the right pane, click in the **Title** box, and then type **Team Leader Blog** In the **URL name** box, type **teamblog** Compare your screen with Figure 1.61.

Figure 1.61

Blog title added

Blog selected

3 In the lower right corner, click **Create**. Take a moment to read the information describing a blog, and then compare your screen with Figure 1.62.

The blog page is created and displays the current date, a *Welcome to your Blog*! announcement, and placeholder text.

Figure 1.62

Current date displays
(yours will differ)

Your name

Placeholder text displays
the Blog Web Part

4 In the upper left corner, click the **Site Actions arrow**, and then click **More Options**. In the center pane, scroll down to the bottom of the list, and then click **Wiki Page Library**. In the *right* pane, click in the **Name** box, and then type **Team Wiki**

5 Click **Create**. Take a moment read the information describing a wiki, and then compare your screen with Figure 1.63.

The Team Wiki page is created and displays.

Figure 1.63

Team Wiki page created

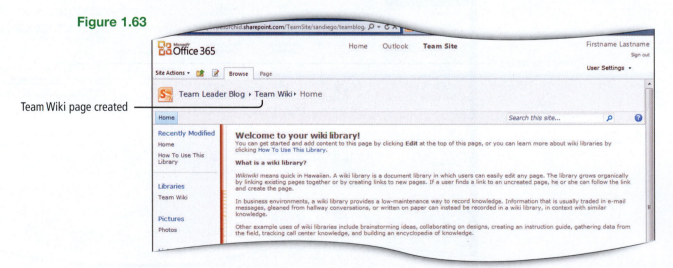

6 Using the technique you have practiced, create a **Window Snip**, click to capture the snip, and then save the snip as a **jpeg** file in your chapter folder. Using your own name, name the file **Lastname_Firstname_1B_Wiki_Snip**

Objective 8 | Survey Team Members

A *survey* is a list of questions that you would like to have people answer. In SharePoint Online, you can create a survey, collect responses, and then view a graphical summary of the responses. Surveys can have a variety of question types, including multiple choice and fill-in-the-blank. Some common question types are shown in the table in Figure 1.64.

Types of Survey Questions

Question Type	Description
Single line of text	The response is confined to a specific number of characters.
Multiple lines of text	The response is confined to a specific number of lines.
Choice	The response is selected from a list of two or more choices.
Rating scale	The response consists of a list of questions with each question rated on a low to high scale—can be a matrix of choices or a Likert scale.
Yes/No	The response is a checkbox, where checked indicates Yes and unchecked indicates No.

Figure 1.64 (TABLE)

Surveys can *branch*—ask different questions depending on the answers given to previous questions.

Activity 1.19 | Creating a Survey

The Bell Orchid management is very attentive to employee opinions. They have asked you to create a survey to help determine the effectiveness of the new San Diego Project Team Site. The Team Site template did not include a survey, so you will add one to the site, and then add questions.

1   On the **Quick Launch**, if necessary, scroll to view the bottom of the list, and then click **All Site Content**. In the upper portion of the screen, click **Create**. In the displayed **Create** dialog box, scroll down as necessary, and then click **Survey.** On the **right**, click in the **Name** box, type **Team Site Feedback** and then compare your screen with Figure 1.65.

Figure 1.65

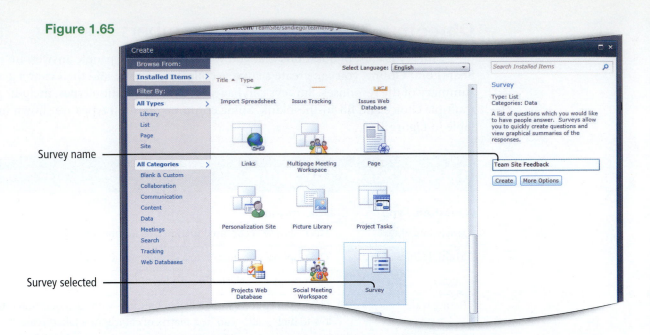

Survey name

Survey selected

2   Click **Create**, and then in the right pane, notice that the text *Type your question here* selected. To replace the selected text, type **Do you use the Team Site?** Under **The type of answer to this question is:** be sure the **Choice (menu to choose from)** option button is selected. Compare your screen with Figure 1.66.

Figure 1.66

Question typed

Question type selected

3   Scroll down as necessary to view, in the middle pane, the area for **Additional Question Settings.** On the right, under **Require a response to this question,** be sure the **No** option button is selected. Under **Enforce unique values,** be sure the **No** option button is selected.

4   Under **Type each choice on a separate line:,** select the text *Enter Choice #1*, type **Yes** and then press Enter. Select the text *Enter Choice #2*, type **No** and then press Enter. Select the text *Enter Choice #3*, and then press Delete.

5   Under **Display choices using:** be sure **Radio Buttons** is selected. Under **Allow 'Fill in' choices,** be sure the **No** option button is selected.

6   Under **Default value,** be sure the **Choice** option button is selected, and then in the box, type **Yes** Compare your screen with Figure 1.67.

Figure 1.67

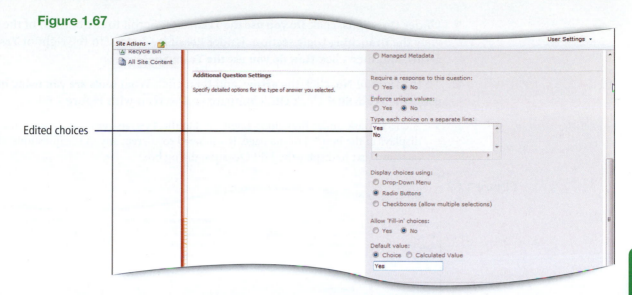

Edited choices

7 Scroll as necessary to the bottom of the page, and then click the **Next Question** button. With the text selected in the **Question** box, type **How do you use the Team Site?** Under **The type of answer to this question is:**, click the **Multiple lines of text** option button.

8 Use the default question settings on the remaining questions, and then scroll down to the bottom of the page and click **Next Question**.

9 In the **Question** box, with the text selected, type **What tools are you using instead of using the Team Site?** Click the **Multiple lines of text** option button. Scroll to the bottom of the page, and then click **Finish**. Compare your screen with Figure 1.68.

The survey questions display at the bottom of the page, in the order they will be delivered. If you need to correct any of the questions, click on the question text to display the Edit Question dialog box again.

Figure 1.68

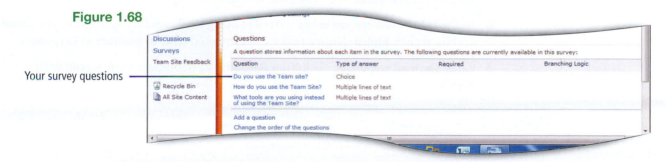

Your survey questions

Activity 1.20 | Adding Branching to a Survey

After all the survey questions are entered, you can add branching. For the Choice question, depending on the answer, an appropriate question should display. For example, if the individual responding to the survey answers *Yes*, then the next question should be *How do you use the Team Site?* If the individual responding to the survey answers *No* to this question, then the next questions should be *What tools are you using instead of using the Team Site?* In this activity, you will set up this branching.

GO! with Office 365 | Chapter 1

1. Under **Questions**, click **Do you use the Team Site?** Scroll to the bottom of the page to view the **Branching Logic** section. Under **Possible Choices**, to the right of **Yes**, click the **arrow**, and then click **How do you use the Team Site?**

2. To the right of **No**, click the **arrow**, and then click **What tools are you using instead of using the Team Site?** Click **OK**. Compare your screen with Figure 1.69.

   A check mark under Branching Logic next to the Yes/No question survey questions displays at the bottom of the page. If you need to correct any of the questions, click on the question text to display the Edit Question dialog box.

Figure 1.69

Indicates branching

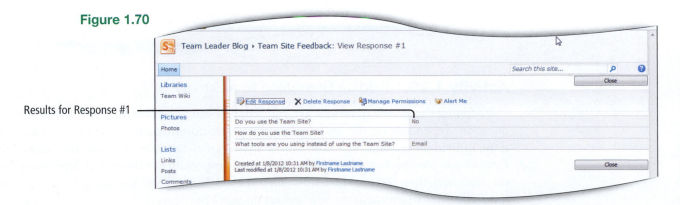

Activity 1.21 | Testing a Survey

Surveys should be tested to ensure that survey takers will see the appropriate questions in the correct order. To test the survey, you will take the survey as if you were a Team member.

1. On the **Quick Launch**, click **Team Site Feedback**. Click **Respond to this Survey**. Under *Do you use the Team Site?*, click **No**, and then click **Next**.

2. In the **What tools are you using instead of using the Team Site?** question, type **Email** and then click **Finish**. Notice that a *1* is displayed next to **Number of Responses**.

3. Click **Show all responses**, click **View Response #1**. Compare your screen with Figure 1.70.

Figure 1.70

Results for Response #1

4 Using the technique you have practiced, create a **Window Snip**, click to capture the snip, and then save the snip as a **jpeg** file in your chapter folder. Using your own name, name the file **Lastname_Firstname_1B_Survey_Snip**

5 Click **Delete Response**, and then click **OK**.

> **Note | Corrections to Survey**
>
> If you need to correct anything on the survey, click on the Team Site Feedback link, click Settings, and then select Survey Settings.

6 In the upper left corner, to the right of **Site Actions**, click the **Navigate Up** button and then click the name of your Team Site to return to the Home page of your Office 365 top-level site.

7 Sign out of your site, and then submit your snip files to your instructor as directed.

End **You have completed Project 1B** ———————————————

Content-Based Assessments

Summary

In this chapter, you explored the four technologies that comprise Microsoft Office 365. You communicated by using Lync Online and used Outlook in an Exchange environment. You also added Web parts to a SharePoint site and used a SharePoint document library. Finally, you created a survey, added branching to a survey, and viewed and exported the survey results.

Key Terms

Matching

Match each term in the second column with its correct definition in the first column by writing the letter of the term on the blank line in front of the correct definition.

_____ 1. A group of workers tasked with working together to solve a problem, make a decision, or create a work product.

_____ 2. Working together with others as a team in an intellectual endeavor to complete a shared task or achieve a shared goal.

_____ 3. A set of secure online services that enables people in an organization to communicate and collaborate by using any Internet-connected device.

_____ 4. The ability to access files and software applications online with multiple devices.

_____ 5. A system that uses controlled servers to ensure the security and privacy of email, to control the storage and use of information, and to protect against the loss of confidential data.

_____ 6. Computers that provide services on a network such as those for email or file storage.

_____ 7. In an Office 365 installation, the person who creates and manages the account, adds new users, sets up the services your organization wants to use, sets permission levels, and manages the SharePoint team sites.

_____ 8. The shortened version of the word *application*.

_____ 9. One of four Outlook indicators associated with your availability for that date and time: Busy, Free, Tentative, or Out of Office.

A App

B Cloud computing

C Collaboration

D Document library

E Free/busy information

F Lync client

G Microsoft Office 365

H Mobile app

I Office 365 Administrator

J Secure environment

K Servers

L Subsites

M Team

N Team site

O Top link bar

_____10. An application that runs on smartphones or tablets and that requires a mobile operating system to run.

_____11. The Microsoft Lync window on a computer.

_____12. A Web site, accessible to those with permission, where a team can organize, author, and share information.

_____13. A storage container—similar to a Windows folder—but with additional functionality and which provides for central storage.

_____14. Additional sites under a team site.

_____15. On a SharePoint site, a series of links at the top of the screen separated by ► symbols to indicate a path from the current site to the sites that are one level below the current site in the hierarchy; each link is an active control that you can click to move directly to the location.

Multiple Choice

Circle the correct answer.

1. A technology that provides email, contacts, calendars, and task scheduling to an organization's employees is:
   A. Exchange Online   **B.** Lync Online   **C.** SharePoint Online

2. A technology that provides instant messaging, audio/video calling, and online meetings is:
   A. Exchange Online   **B.** Lync Online   **C.** SharePoint Online

3. A technology that provides document sharing and team sites to share documents with others, manage documents, and publish reports for others to see is:
   A. Exchange Online   **B.** Lync Online   **C.** SharePoint Online

4. The online companions to the desktop versions of Microsoft Office Word, Excel, PowerPoint, and OneNote are known as:
   A. Office Web Apps   **B.** Lync Online   **C.** Office 365

5. A mini-application or module that displays information on a page or performs a special function is a:
   A. Web part   **B.** blog   **C.** wiki

6. A page that stores information by topic is a:
   A. Web part   **B.** blog   **C.** wiki

7. An online journal is a:
   A. Web part   **B.** blog   **C.** wiki

8. A computer program installed on a hard drive and that requires an operating system to run is a:
   A. mobile app   **B.** desktop app   **C.** Web app

9. An application that you run from the Web instead of your hard drive is a:
   A. mobile app   **B.** desktop app   **C.** Web app

10. A view that enables you to see email threads in Outlook in a condensed format is:
    A. conversation view   **B.** desktop app   **C.** Web app

Glossary

App The shortened version of the word *application*.

At sign (@) The symbol used to separate the user name and domain name of an email address.

Basic Meeting Workspace A site to plan, organize, and capture the results of a meeting; it provides lists for managing the agenda, meeting attendees, and documents.

Blogs Online journals.

Branch In a survey, to ask different questions depending on the answers given to previous questions.

Cloud computing The ability to access files and software applications online with multiple devices.

Collaboration Working together with others as a team in an intellectual endeavor to complete a shared task or achieve a shared goal.

Contacts Coworkers, customers, suppliers, friends, and family members with whom you communicate.

Conversation View A view that enables you to see email threads in a condensed format.

Desktop app A computer program that is installed on the hard drive of your computer and that requires a computer operating system like Windows 7 to run.

Document library A storage container—similar to a Windows folder—but with additional functionality and which provides for central storage.

Domain name The host name of a recipient's mail server.

Form An Outlook window for displaying and collecting information; there are forms for messages, contacts, tasks, and appointments.

Free/busy information One of four Outlook indicators associated with your availability for that date and time: Busy, Free, Tentative, or Out of Office.

IMAP IMAP is a protocol that creates folders on a server to store and organize messages for retrieval by other computers.

Inbox In Outlook, the folder in which incoming mail is stored.

List A collection of similar items such as contact information or inventory items.

Lync client The Microsoft Lync window on a computer.

Microsoft Exchange Online Provides email, contacts, calendars, and task scheduling to an organization's employees.

Microsoft Lync Online The instant messaging, audio/video calling, and online meeting tool in Office 365.

Microsoft Office 365 A set of secure online services that enables people in an organization to communicate and collaborate by using any Internet-connected device.

Microsoft SharePoint Online Provides document sharing and team sites to share documents with others in an organization, manage documents, and publish reports for others to see.

Mobile app An application that runs on smartphones or tablets and that requires a mobile operating system to run.

Office 365 Administrator The person who creates and manages the account, adds new users, sets up the services your organization wants to use, sets permission levels, and manages the SharePoint team sites.

Office Web Apps The online companions to the desktop versions of Microsoft Office Word, Excel, PowerPoint, and OneNote that enable you to create, access, share, and perform light editing on Microsoft Office documents from any device that connects to the Internet and uses a supported Web browser.

Permissions Access rights that define the ability of an individual or group to view or make changes to documents.

Personal information manager An application such as Outlook that enables you to store information about your contacts and also enables you keep track of your daily schedule, tasks to complete, and meetings to attend.

POP3 A common protocol used to retrieve email messages from an Internet email server.

Quick Launch A column of links on the left side of a SharePoint site with which you can navigate to important content in the current site; for example lists and libraries.

Secure environment A system that uses controlled servers to ensure the security and privacy of email, to control the storage and use of information, and to protect against the loss of confidential data.

Servers Computers that provide services on a network such as an email server or a file server.

Site collection A group of Web sites within your Office 365 installation that has the same owner and shares administrative settings such as permissions.

Subsite Additional sites under a team site.

Survey A list of questions that you would like to have people answer.

Team A group of workers tasked with working together to solve a problem, make a decision, or create a work product.

Team site A Web site, accessible to those with permission, where a team can organize, author, and share information.

Top link bar On a SharePoint site, a series of links at the top of the screen separated by ▶ symbols to indicate a path from the current site to the sites that are one level below the current site in the hierarchy; each link is an active control that you can click to move directly to the location.

Views Ways to look at similar information in different formats and arrangements.

Web app Another name for a Web-based application.

Web browser Software, such as Internet Explorer, Firefox, Safari, or Chrome, that displays Web pages.

Web Part A mini-application or module that displays information on a page or performs a special function.

Web-based application An application that is not installed on your computer; for the application to run, it requires that you use Web browser software such as Internet Explorer, Firefox, Chrome, or Safari.

Wikis Pages that store information by topic.

Windows Live SkyDrive A free Web-based application with which you can save, store, organize, and share files online.

Index

DATE DUE

PRINTED IN U.S.A.